YOU ARE
Endlessly Loved

YOU ARE *Endlessly Loved*

Encouraging Devotions for Women

RAE SIMONS

BARBOUR
PUBLISHING

ISBN 979-8-89151-080-7

Previously published as *God Calls You Loved*, published by Barbour Publishing.

Published by Barbour Publishing, Inc., 1810 Barbour Drive, Uhrichsville, Ohio 44683, www.barbourbooks.com

Our mission is to inspire the world with the life-changing message of the Bible.

Member of the Evangelical Christian Publishers Association

Printed in China.

INTRODUCTION

The Bible says that we have a loving God, and then it goes even further and says, "God *is* love" (1 John 4:8, 16, emphasis added). These are wonderful, comforting words, and yet as human beings, we'll never be able to fully understand what the love of God means. By nature, God is too immense for our human minds to comprehend—and so is His love.

But although you'll never fully understand God's love, you *can* experience it. A good place to start is with the words of the Bible, allowing them to settle in your mind. That's what this book does: it gives you a brief Bible passage that describes some aspect of God's love for you. Next, you can spend a few moments meditating on the message of the passage, allowing it to take root in your mind. Finally, you can respond in prayer, turning your time with the Bible into a two-way conversation with the Lord. This book gives you this three-part structure as a place to build your love relationship with God. Each just-right-sized devotion is an opportunity to soak in the Lord's love and care for you.

What comes next is up to you. As you daily apply God's Word to your life, you make more and more room for God's love to flow—both into your own heart and then out from you to touch others. God's love will change you, like yeast inside bread dough. It becomes active. It reaches out and changes the world.

God loves *you* so much—and He wants to use you to carry His message of love to others.

FOR GOD SO LOVED

For God so loved the world that he gave his one and only Son, that whoever believes in him shall not perish but have eternal life. For God did not send his Son into the world to condemn the world, but to save the world through him.

JOHN 3:16–17 NIV

You may have learned John 3:16 when you were a child. It's one of the most memorized verses in the Bible. Some of us have heard it so many times that we no longer stop to think what it really means. But when you stop to truly think about it, it's pretty amazing—God, the Creator of the universe, loves you so much that He gave His Son to come to our world, be born as a human being just like you, and then die—all so you could live forever with God in eternity. Humanity's greatest fear, the fear of death, has been removed by the love of God. The whole purpose of Jesus' coming to earth wasn't to tell you how sinful you are; it was to save you from death—because He loves you that much.

Thank You, Creator God, for sending Jesus. Thank You, Jesus, for being willing to live and die for me. Thank You that I no longer have to be afraid of death, because I will live forever with You. Thank You for loving me so much.

UNEARNED

God demonstrates his own love for us in this:
While we were still sinners, Christ died for us.
ROMANS 5:8 NIV

Do you ever feel as though you have to earn God's love? When you know you've strayed away from God's path for you, do you avoid prayer? Do you keep your head down, spiritually speaking, hoping God won't notice you?

You don't need to! God doesn't want you to make yourself into a good person before you come to Him. He doesn't ask that you earn His love by obeying all His rules. God loves you just the way you are—and Jesus was willing to die for you just the way you are. He loves you unconditionally. You don't have to do one single thing to earn His love.

So if you know you've strayed away from God, talk to Him about it. Be honest with Him, knowing that His love is always there, no matter how you may have messed up. Don't cut yourself off from God. He's longing to hear your voice.

Thank You, Jesus, that I don't have to do anything to earn Your love. I'm so grateful that You gave Yourself for me—and that You continue to give Yourself to me every day, every moment. Forgive me for the times I shut You out of my life. Thank You for Your unconditional love.

FRIENDS WITH JESUS

"I'm no longer calling you servants because servants don't understand what their master is thinking and planning. No, I've named you friends because I've let you in on everything I've heard from the Father."
JOHN 15:15 MSG

Do you feel like God's servant, someone who's expected to obey orders? Someone who's told what to do but doesn't really know what's going on? Jesus doesn't want you to feel that way. He loves you so much that He wants you to think of Him as your friend—because that's the way He thinks of you. As His friend.

That's pretty amazing to think about. Jesus, the Christ, the Son of God, wants to be your friend. He wants you to share your life with Him, the way friends do—and He wants to share His life with you. He doesn't want you to feel like a servant. No, instead, He wants you to know that you're His beloved friend. He wants there to be love and trust and intimacy between the two of you. He longs for you to have so much confidence in His love and friendship that you can talk to Him about anything.

Jesus, I know You are the best friend I could ever have, someone I can trust absolutely. Human friends can't help but let each other down sometimes, but You'll never let me down. I can depend on You. Help me to be the kind of friend to You that You can depend on too.

NO GREATER LOVE

"There is no greater love than to lay down one's life for one's friends."
JOHN 15:13 NLT

Would you die for your friends? Do you think they would die for you? Friends who truly love each other are willing to give their lives for one another. Thankfully, though, we're seldom asked to actually die for our friends. But do we do something that's sometimes even harder—do we lay down our own selfishness on behalf of our friends? Are we willing to be inconvenienced by them? Would we set aside our own desires to help our friends when they're in need?

That's the kind of friend you have in Jesus. Not only did He actually, literally die for you, He continues to lay down His life on your behalf, every day, from the moment you were born until the moment you pass out of this life into eternity. He gives Himself totally to you, holding nothing back. His friendship has no limits.

And one day, in eternity, you'll get to explore that friendship even further. You'll see Him face-to-face—and you'll finally be able to truly understand how much He's given you.

Jesus, thank You that You laid down Your life for me. You accepted a painful death on the cross for me. But You didn't stop there. You keep on giving Yourself to me. You give me the gift of Your life eternally. I can't really understand what that means—but help me to understand more than I do now. I want our friendship to grow.

A TWO-WAY STREET

This is how we know what love is: Jesus Christ laid down his life for us. And we ought to lay down our lives for our brothers and sisters.

1 JOHN 3:16 NIV

We use the word *love* in so many ways. We fall in love. We love chocolate. We love summer days and new clothes and our favorite authors. But the Bible makes clear that the kind of love it's talking about is different. Jesus shows us this kind of love. He gave His life for us. That's the love God is talking about when He says He loves you.

But true love should be reciprocal. It's a two-way street. So how can you show God you return His love? By loving others. When you love the people in your life, when you put them first, ahead of your own selfish wants, you're showing God that you love Him. When you love others the way Jesus loves you, you're reciprocating God's love. You're taking part in a relationship of love that just keeps expanding, including everyone with whom you come in contact.

Christ, living Lord, I want You to know how much I love You. Teach me to love others the way You love me. Give me the strength to lay down my life the way You laid down Your life for me. May my love for You spill out into the entire world around me.

GOD'S LOVE NEVER QUITS

You, O God, are both tender and kind, not easily angered, immense in love, and you never, never quit.
PSALM 86:15 MSG

As human beings, we can get tired of loving. Our strength is limited, and loving can be exhausting. People don't always make it easy to love them. They can be annoying and unreasonable and even cruel. Sometimes we just want to quit loving altogether. It's the only way we can see to protect our hearts. (Of course, love does set boundaries. It doesn't let people abuse us or take advantage of us. That's not good for us, and it's not good for the other person either.) Fortunately, God's love never gets tired. He doesn't get irritated when you make the same mistake for the hundredth time. His love is immense, so wide and deep that you'll never reach the end of it. His kindness and tenderness are never exhausted, and He never gets discouraged with you. His love for you never, never quits.

Loving God, I thank You for Your immense and endless love. I can't really imagine how much You love me. It's hard to believe the lengths to which You'll go to show me Your love. But I want to experience more and more of Your love in my life. I want to head out like an explorer into the ceaseless depths of Your love for me.

GOD IS GOOD!

Give thanks to the Lord, for he is good! His faithful love endures forever.
1 Chronicles 16:34 NLT

We all know that God is good. But what do we really mean when we say something is good? A "good cookie" is a cookie that pleases our sense of taste. A "good book" holds our interest and perhaps moves us to both tears and laughter. A "good idea" is one that's both unique and practical; it's something that will bring positive results. And then we come to a "good person," and things get a little trickier. Our first impulse may be to say that a good person doesn't do "bad" things; she doesn't commit sins such as lying, stealing, or murder. But notice that we didn't do this with any of the other things to which we applied the word *good*. We didn't say that a good cookie doesn't taste yucky, or that a good book isn't boring, or that a good idea isn't stupid. So how can we define a "good person" more positively? By saying that a good person is kind, a good person acts in love, a good person goes out of their way to help others.

And those are all the characteristics that apply to the God who loves you. Like a cookie, His taste is sweet; like a good book, He's capable of holding your attention endlessly; and like a good idea, He brings positive results into the world. But even more than that, He is kind, He always acts in love, and He goes out of His way to help you.

Thank You, Lord, for Your goodness.

PERFECT LOVE

Perfect love expels all fear. If we are afraid, it is for fear of punishment, and this shows that we have not fully experienced his perfect love.
1 JOHN 4:18 NLT

The Bible talks about the "fear of the Lord"—but that doesn't mean that God wants us to be afraid of Him. We're to feel awe in His presence, but not fear, because, as John the author of this verse knew, fear doubts the reality of love. When we're talking to someone, we may feel anxious and uncertain if we suspect the other person doesn't like us. We may feel nervous standing up in front of a crowd of people who regard us with scorn. But when we're with someone who we know loves us, we feel perfectly relaxed. We're secure. We can be ourselves, knowing that we are accepted and loved.

That's how God wants you to feel whenever you come into His presence. You don't need to be nervous that He's angry with you about something. You don't need to be scared that He's going to punish you. You can relax, knowing that His love for you is perfect. Nothing can diminish it or take it away.

Thank You, God, that Your love for me is perfect.
Help me never to fear You—and always to trust Your love.

DON'T DESPAIR!

"Don't be afraid. Dear Zion, don't despair. Your God is present among you, a strong Warrior there to save you. Happy to have you back, he'll calm you with his love and delight you with his songs."
ZEPHANIAH 3:16–17 MSG

We all mess up. We do the things we know aren't pleasing to God. We hurt others, we hurt ourselves, and we hurt the God who loves us. But what then? Do we get discouraged and give up? Do we decide, "What's the point of trying to follow Jesus when, sooner or later, I always do something wrong?"

Those feelings are normal, human reactions to failure. We've all had them. But God doesn't want you to give up on yourself, because He never will. No matter what you've done, He's always eager to take you back—not so He can scold you, but so He can sing His love songs to you.

God, it's hard for me to believe how much You love me. I can't comprehend Your love. All I can do is say thank You.

NEVER FORSAKEN

You are a God of forgiveness, gracious and compassionate, slow to anger and abounding in mercy; and You did not abandon them.

NEHEMIAH 9:17 NASB

Have you ever been abandoned? It's a painful experience. Whether it's a spouse, a friend, a parent, a sibling, or a child, nothing hurts more than having someone you love turn their back on you. When that happens, we may be completely innocent, and we may never understand what happened. Other times though, we know deep in our hearts that we were at fault. But that doesn't make the rejection hurt any less.

The good thing about God's love is this: it doesn't matter what you do—He'll never reject you. No matter how many times you turn your back on Him, He forgives you instantly as soon as you turn back to Him. He abounds in mercy. He is full of compassion. He'll never abandon you!

Thank You, Lord, that You are a God of forgiveness, a God of grace and compassion. Thank You for Your mercy. I'm so grateful that You will never abandon me.

GOD'S LAVISH LOVE

"I lavish unfailing love to a thousand generations.
I forgive iniquity, rebellion, and sin."
EXODUS 34:7 NLT

God loves you. You've probably heard that hundreds of times. But has it really sunk in? Do you truly understand that God's love for you isn't some small, obligatory thing? That it's not just some words that don't mean very much? No, God's love for you is real. It's practical. He expresses His love to you every day, in a thousand different ways.

God's love is immense in scope. It's lavish, brimming with abundance. And it's so great that it isn't limited to your life only. No, it spills from your life, flowing through you out into the world and into the future. Just imagine it! God's love not only fills your own life to the brim; it also reaches forward in time for a thousand generations. There's no limit to God's love—and there's no limit to His forgiveness.

Thank You, God, for Your lavish love. I don't understand how You can love me so much—and yet Your Word tells me over and over and over again that You do. Even when I rebel, even when I let sin come between me and You, Your love for me never ends. It just keeps going. It never fails.

HUNGER AND THIRST

Let them give thanks to the Lord for His faithful love and His wonderful works for all humanity. For He has satisfied the thirsty and filled the hungry with good things.

Psalm 107:8–9 HCSB

Do you ever feel as though something inside you is hungry? As though you're yearning for something to fill up a hole inside you, an empty, aching place? Or maybe you feel as though you're thirsting to death, craving something that will quench the longing within your heart. You might have tried to satisfy those empty feelings with other things—things like food, or shopping, or romance, or work, or having fun—but nothing really works. You feel a little better for a while, but then that same hungry, thirsty feeling is back again.

God understands that feeling. In fact, God is the one who put it there inside you—but He put it there because He knows He's the only one who can truly satisfy it. Your heart was made for God, and without Him, you'll always feel as though you're missing something in your life. Only God's love can satisfy your hungry heart.

Dear Lord, I've been hungry for Your presence. I've been thirsty for Your love. I keep trying to find other things to fill me up inside, but nothing works. I don't know why I'd try, when You're offering me Your love—and I can have as much of it as I want. Thank You that there are no limits to Your love.

SKY HIGH

Your love, Lord, reaches to the heavens, your faithfulness to the skies.
Psalm 36:5 NIV

Have you ever lain on your back on the ground and looked up at a starry sky? All those countless stars, a vast and endless universe, stretched out across the nighttime sky. Our brains can't comprehend the infinity of space, the boundless reaches of the universe. When we try to grasp something so immense, our minds boggle. They just can't reach that far. They can't even imagine something so wide and deep, without boundaries.

God's love for you is even more enormous than the universe. It is limitless. No matter how far you reached, you could never come to the end of His love or His faithfulness. Even if you could measure the sky, you could never measure God's love. God's great and faithful love reaches into forever. He loves you that much!

Lord, each time I look up at the sky, may it be like a love letter from You to me, a reminder of how vast Your love for me is. Thank You for loving me so much, so faithfully. I can't comprehend Your love—but I am so grateful that it's real. Thank You for giving me a universe full of love.

DELIGHT

How priceless is your unfailing love, O God! People take refuge in the shadow of your wings. They feast on the abundance of your house; you give them drink from your river of delights. For with you is the fountain of life; in your light we see light.

PSALM 36:7–9 NIV

Sometimes God's love doesn't seem very real. It seems like something to talk about in church—but not something to fill your life. It may seem like something small, unimportant, even a little boring.

But the reality of God's love is very different. It's like the best feast you've ever tasted. There's nothing small or stingy about it; it's rich with abundance. It's an endless river of joy flooding into your life, bringing to life each aspect of your being. In fact, God's love is the source of all life, a fountain that is constantly flowing, bringing new things into being. And His love is the light that allows us to see all of life; His love gives clarity and insight.

The word that perhaps best describes God's love—*delight*!

God, I could never put a price on Your love. Everywhere I turn, I see Your love at work in my life. You are my refuge, my home, my fountain of life, my light. You are my delight!

EXTRAVAGANT LOVE

Watch what God does, and then you do it, like children who learn proper behavior from their parents. Mostly what God does is love you. Keep company with him and learn a life of love. Observe how Christ loved us. His love was not cautious but extravagant. He didn't love in order to get something from us but to give everything of himself to us.

Ephesians 5:1–2 MSG

As human beings, most of us have been hurt enough in our lives that we're often careful about how much of our hearts we give away. We don't want to risk being hurt again, so we play it safe. We're cautious.

But that's not how God loves. Again and again, the Bible uses words like "extravagant" to describe God's love. God holds nothing back. He gives His entire self to you.

And as you keep company with God, you'll learn to love more like He loves. You'll no longer worry about being hurt. You'll know that even if people let you down, God never will. Love is what He is. It's what He does.

Jesus, thank You for showing me what love looks like. I want to learn from You. I want a life of love. You give me everything, all of You. Help me now to give myself away—to You and to others, just as You give Yourself to me.

BELOVED CHILD

See what great love the Father has lavished on us, that we should be called children of God! And that is what we are!

1 JOHN 3:1 NIV

Here it is again: the Bible once more describes the love of God as lavish, extravagant, immense. This theme is woven through the Bible from beginning to end. It's as though God were trying to say the same thing in as many ways as possible, so that you finally get the message—God loves you!

He loves you the way a good parent loves a beloved child—with gentleness, commitment, devotion, tenderness, and constant care. But God doesn't only love you *like* a good parent. God *is* your parent. He is your Father, and the Bible also says God loves you the way a mother loves. It's not make-believe. It's not just pretty language. It's reality. You are the beloved child of God. You really are.

Father God, thank You for lavishing Your love on me. I am so grateful that I can call You Father. When life looks bleak, when I feel discouraged or anxious or full of doubt, remind me that no matter what happens, I am Your beloved child.

GOD IS LOVE

Everyone who loves is born of God and experiences a relationship with God. The person who refuses to love doesn't know the first thing about God, because God is love—so you can't know him if you don't love. This is how God showed his love for us: God sent his only Son into the world so we might live through him. This is the kind of love we are talking about—not that we once upon a time loved God, but that he loved us and sent his Son as a sacrifice to clear away our sins and the damage they've done to our relationship with God.

1 John 4:7–10 MSG

Every loving human relationship is a little glimpse of God, for it is through loving others that we begin to see God. God is present in our love for one another. When we open up our hearts to others, we make room for God to come in too.

But if we shut ourselves off from others, if we treat others with disrespect or even just indifference, then there's no point in trying to say we have a relationship with God. If we don't love other people, we can't love God either. The two things go together.

God shows us what real love looks like. It looks like Jesus.

Thank You, God, for loving me before I even had any idea who You were. Thank You that You loved me so much that You sent Jesus. I'm so glad that because of Jesus, I can come close to You.

GOD'S BANNER

He brought me to the banqueting house, and his banner over me was love.
SONG OF SOLOMON 2:4 KJV

Imagine the scene. God, the Creator of the universe, has invited you to a banquet He's holding to celebrate His love for you. You are His honored guest. The sun is shining, the grass is green and full of flowers, and a bright banner flies from the top of the banquet house. As it flutters in the breeze, you realize that the banner is the expression of God's feelings for you.

In ancient times, when a king rode into battle, he carried a banner that floated high above his warriors' heads. That way they would always know where he was. The banner would guide them and bring them back to him, even in the midst of the battle's chaos. The banner flying over you is love. And this love streams out over your life, showing you where you can find the presence of God.

This may seem like a fairy tale or a scene out of a romance novel. The entire Song of Solomon is, in fact, a romance—it's the romance between God and His beloved. As you read it, one thing is clear: God loves you passionately. He adores you with all His heart. His banner over you is love.

Thank You, God, that I am Your beloved.

SPRING IS COMING

My beloved spoke and said to me, "Arise, my darling, my beautiful one, come with me. See! The winter is past; the rains are over and gone. Flowers appear on the earth; the season of singing has come, the cooing of doves is heard in our land. The fig tree forms its early fruit; the blossoming vines spread their fragrance. Arise, come, my darling; my beautiful one, come with me."

Song of Solomon 2:10–13 NIV

Hard times come to all of us. Just as summer always cools into autumn, followed by the icy winter with its long hours of darkness, so happy times never last forever. But neither do the hard times. Even the longest winter comes to an end. And God's love remains steady through the turning cycles of our lives.

If you've been living in a phase of your life that seems as bleak as winter, hear God's voice calling to you now, telling you that better times lie ahead. Because He loves you so much, He delights to shower your life with blessings—bright blossoms, singing birds, and trees laden with fruit. "Come see!" God is calling to you. "See, My darling, My beautiful one, what I have in store for you."

Beloved God, it's hard for me to believe that You love me so much. When my life is hard, I wonder if You really love me at all. Help me to trust You more. Teach me that in summer or winter, spring or autumn, Your love for me never fails.

INVINCIBLE LOVE

Love is invincible facing danger and death. Passion laughs at the terrors of hell. The fire of love stops at nothing—it sweeps everything before it. Flood waters can't drown love, torrents of rain can't put it out.
Song of Solomon 8:6–7 MSG

Lovers dare things that others might not try. Their love gives them courage to face the future together, no matter what lies ahead. "Through sickness and health," they promise, "for richer and for poorer."

Sometimes, though, human love does fail. But God's love never does. It is unfazed by danger, by death, by hell itself. Like a mighty forest fire, it sweeps through your life, igniting everything with its fire and light, and nothing—not a flood of water, not a torrential downpour—can extinguish it.

So if you think you've done something to block God's love from reaching you, know that's not possible. God's love is the most powerful force in the universe—and you are God's beloved. He won't let anything hinder His love from reaching you.

God, when I read how much You love me, I'm a little overwhelmed. I don't feel worthy of so much love. I'm afraid I'll let You down. I worry I can't live up to what You ask of me. When I feel like that, Lord, remind me that nothing stops Your love.

BELOVED

My beloved is mine, and I am his.
Song of Solomon 2:16 KJV

As you read verses from Song of Solomon, does it seem a little strange to you that God would use the language of romance to describe His feelings for you? We call God Father, and we think of ourselves as God's children. We read in the Bible that God feels mother-love for us, and we hear Jesus saying that He calls us His friends. Those relationships all help us to understand a little more about the way God loves us. To call God our lover, however, may seem uncomfortable. And yet every human love relationship reflects some aspect of God's love for you. This most intimate of human loves, the love between lovers, also reveals how God feels about you.

Just as lovers belong to each other, so you and God belong together. Your hearts are sealed together—not by a sense of duty or guilt but by love. You are God's beloved. You belong to Him. And He belongs to you.

Beloved Lord, I can't comprehend how much You love me. I hear You calling me to a relationship so deep I can't even imagine what it will be like. But I have not only my entire lifetime to learn to love You; I have all eternity.

GOD'S DESIRE

I belong to my love, and his desire is for me.
SONG OF SOLOMON 7:10 HCSB

Lovers long for each other. When they're separated, missing each other is painful. It's hard to go about normal life when the only thing they can think about is the person they love most in all the world.

God also desires you that way. When you've separated yourself from Him, His heart aches for you, missing your presence with Him. He feels lonely for you. He yearns for the day when your hearts will be reunited. Nothing can *really* separate you from His love—but you can decide to turn away, to hide yourself in places where you won't feel God's presence with you. When you do that, God suffers. He waits eagerly for the day you'll come back to Him.

Like a human lover, God longs to be your beloved. He desires for you to give yourself to Him, completely and utterly and forever.

God, please forgive me for the times I run away from You, the times I put up walls around my heart, trying to shut You out. I know You give me Your entire self, holding nothing back. Make me more like You.

CHRIST'S LIFE IN YOU

My old self has been crucified with Christ. It is no longer I who live, but Christ lives in me. So I live in this earthly body by trusting in the Son of God, who loved me and gave himself for me.

GALATIANS 2:20 NLT

When you read about the vastness of God's love, it can be overwhelming. You may wonder, *How can I possibly measure up to a love so immense?* But don't worry. You don't have to do it all by yourself. You have help.

Christ, who loves you so much that He gives Himself to you, lives in you. He is a part of your inmost self, the secret part of you deep inside. You're still you of course, still walking around in your same body; but at the same time, Christ is there within you, helping you, loving you from the inside out. The selfish person you used to be is no longer running the show.

And as you make more room for Christ, He helps you grow into the person you were always meant to be—a strong, courageous, joyful person who's capable of loving God with all her heart.

Christ Jesus, thank You that You love me so much that You give me Yourself. Help my selfishness to die so that You have room to live inside me. I know I'm only human, but I'm trusting You to change me. I want to be like You.

RECIPROCATED LOVE

I will declare that your love stands firm forever,
that you have established your faithfulness in heaven itself.
PSALM 89:2 NIV

Love affairs are meant to be reciprocal. Something is wrong if one person is always saying, "I love you," while the other person never speaks those words. A romance is lopsided and unhealthy if only one person expresses love, whether with words or with countless thoughtful acts, both big and small. A one-sided relationship can't grow. It doesn't really go anywhere, because it takes two to make a relationship thrive.

The same is true of your love relationship with God. Again and again throughout the Bible, He tells you that He loves you. He fills your life with blessings, His love tokens to you. Now it's your turn. Speak out. Tell the world about God's love and faithfulness. Letting others know about God's eternal love is one way to let Him know that His love for you is reciprocated. It's mutual!

Lord of love, I want to show You how much I love You,
so I'm going to tell the world how amazing You are.
I don't want our relationship to be one-sided. I want to do
whatever it takes to make this relationship thrive and grow.

MAKE LOVE A SONG

I will sing of the graciousness of the LORD forever; to all generations I will make Your faithfulness known with my mouth.

PSALM 89:1 NASB

When we really fall in love, we don't usually have to work hard to tell others about our feelings. Instead, it's like a song that's constantly singing inside our hearts. It spills out of us naturally, effortlessly. And that's how it should be with God too. Telling others about His love shouldn't be a solemn, joyless duty. It should be something joyful, something that leaps out of us, like a song we can't stop singing.

Notice that the Bible says this song will be heard by all generations. Your peers need to hear about God's love. Children need to learn to sing God's love songs from the time they are very small. And older people need to be reminded that God's love will never forsake them. Your song of love will even spill into the future, down through the generations, shaping the lives of people who are not yet born, people you will never know in this life. That's how powerful love can be!

God, I want to learn Your love songs so I can sing them out loud and clear for absolutely everyone to hear.

A LOVE-FILLED WORLD

O Lord, your unfailing love fills the earth.
Psalm 119:64 NLT

The Bible is full of God's love promises—but His expressions of love aren't limited to His Word. They jump out everywhere you turn. In fact, His love is so great that it fills the whole world. If you have eyes to see, you'll begin to notice His love tokens sprinkled throughout your life, from morning till night.

The sun shining is a sign of God's love and care. So is the rain that refreshes the earth. A friend's listening ear, a child's smile, a beautiful sunset, a delicious meal, a good book, the scent of new-mown grass, flowers growing along the road, a cat's purr—all these are expressions of God's love. When you look back at your life, recognizing the path that got you where you are today, you can see it was God's hand that guided you in love, even when you were unaware. God's unfailing love is woven through your entire life.

God of love, thank You that Your love never fails. And thank You that Your love for me flows through every moment of my life. I know some days I'm so busy or worried or upset about something that I overlook Your messages of love. Remind me to pay attention.

GOD IS ON YOUR SIDE

What shall we say about such wonderful things as these? If God is for us, who can ever be against us? Since he did not spare even his own Son but gave him up for us all, won't he also give us everything else?

ROMANS 8:31–32 NLT

Does it ever feel as though the whole world is against you? Nothing goes right. Everyone else seems to have all the luck, while you're stumbling around in the dark. We all have days (or weeks or months) when we feel like that. But the truth is, God is always, always on your side. So who cares if the world *is* against you (though it probably isn't)?

It's easy to worry about the future, about the things we hear on the news, about money, or about the health and well-being of our loved ones. But God gave us His own Son, a part of His very self. He's not going to hold anything else back from you. He's making sure you have everything you truly need. You can count on Him. He's on your side.

Thank You, loving Lord, for giving me everything, even Your Son. When I worry and fret, remind me that You are on my side. I can rely on You to take care of me. Through thick and thin, You'll be with me.

NO MORE GUILT

Who dares accuse us whom God has chosen for his own? No one—for God himself has given us right standing with himself. Who then will condemn us? No one—for Christ Jesus died for us and was raised to life for us, and he is sitting in the place of honor at God's right hand, pleading for us.

ROMANS 8:33–34 NLT

Guilt can be a heavy burden to carry. We all have a load of shame and guilt, because we've all done things that hurt others, said things we wished we hadn't, and acted in ways that we regret later. It's easy to let the guilt and shame we feel weigh us down. Guilt can rob us of our joy and make us anxious. Shame can make us hate ourselves.

Those feelings don't come from God, though. God doesn't want anything, including guilt, to come between you and His love. Jesus has made things right between you and God—and God does not condemn you for the mistakes you've made in the past. Instead, He holds out His hand, asking only that you walk more closely with Him in the future.

Lord, I'm so sorry for all the sins I've committed. I wish I could undo them, but I can't. I feel so guilty—but I'm giving my guilt to You. Take it from me and replace it with confidence in Your love. Walk with me, helping me to deal with the consequences of my actions. Thank You that You don't condemn. Your love is unconditional.

WHEN TROUBLE COMES

Does it mean he no longer loves us if we have trouble or calamity, or are persecuted, or hungry, or destitute, or in danger, or threatened with death? . . . No, despite all these things, overwhelming victory is ours through Christ, who loved us.

ROMANS 8:35, 37 NLT

With so many promises in the Bible about God's love and blessing, it's hard to understand what's going on when trouble comes into your life. You may wonder, *Was God lying? Is the Bible false? Does God not love me after all?*

Paul, the author of this verse of scripture, understood those feelings—and he wanted to make sure that people understood that God's love never leaves us. Life is full of trouble and heartache, and hard times come to all of us sooner or later. But when that happens, God is still with us, and He still loves us.

Think about a marriage between two people. No matter how much they love each other, they are bound to experience some pain in their lives together. That pain doesn't mean their love is false. Instead, they can go through the pain together, supporting each other. If they can do that, then their love will grow stronger and stronger.

That's the kind of relationship God wants to have with you. When times are hard, He wants you to draw even closer to Him.

Lord Jesus, even when trouble comes, I ask that You give me victory through Your love.

NOTHING

For I am convinced that neither death, nor life, nor angels, nor principalities, nor things present, nor things to come, nor powers, nor height, nor depth, nor any other created thing will be able to separate us from the love of God that is in Christ Jesus our Lord.

ROMANS 8:38–39 NASB

Did you ever read *The Runaway Bunny* by Margaret Wise Brown? In this children's book, the little bunny keeps trying to run away, to all sorts of places—but wherever he goes, his mother follows him. Nothing can separate the little bunny from his mother's love.

The same is true of God. Nothing can come between you and His love. Not your worries about the future, not your guilt about the past, not the government, not the powers of evil, not even death itself can separate you from God. Even your own runaway heart can't do it—because wherever you go, just like the runaway bunny's mother, God will follow you. He won't let anything get in the way of His love for you.

Thank You, loving Lord, that You follow me wherever I go. I can never stray where Your love can't reach me. But I don't want to run from You any longer. I want to turn around and run straight into Your arms.

THE POWER OF LOVE

God hath not given us the spirit of fear;
but of power, and of love, and of a sound mind.
2 TIMOTHY 1:7 KJV

It has been said that worry is like negative prayer—instead of dwelling on God's love and promises, we dwell on all that is negative in life. Instead of asking for God's blessings, we imagine all that might go wrong. But worry is never productive. It doesn't make us better able to face the future. Instead, it robs us of our strength—physically, emotionally, and spiritually. It steals our confidence in God, in ourselves, and in others. It makes us lie awake imagining worst-case scenarios, rather than resting in God's love.

God doesn't want your mind to be filled with anxious thoughts. He wants to replace that spirit of fear with His own Spirit, filling you up with power, love, and a stable mind.

Dear God, I give You my worries. I know I'll probably keep taking them back from You, but when that happens, please just remind me to give them back to You all over again. Fill me with Your Spirit.

EARTHQUAKES

"Even if the mountains walk away and the hills
fall to pieces, my love won't walk away from you,
my covenant commitment of peace won't fall apart."
The God who has compassion on you says so.

Isaiah 54:10 MSG

Have you ever been in an earthquake? It's a terrifying experience. We take for granted that the earth under our feet is solid, dependable. To have it start shaking, to have buildings sway and crash, is horrifying. The aftermath of an earthquake, where everything is changed, is nearly as frightening.

Sometimes the earthquakes in our lives aren't actual geological events. Instead, something we've been depending on falls to pieces. It could be a marriage, a friendship, or a job. Or the upheaval could be caused by a death or other circumstances. However it happens, it's an unnerving experience. It's hard to believe something so horrible could happen; our minds keep telling us it just isn't possible. Nothing looks the way it did before. We lack the confidence we need to move forward; we're too afraid of the aftershocks. It's difficult to trust again.

But whether the earthquakes in your life are actual or circumstantial, God's love for you remains steady. No matter what happens, He'll be there with you.

I am so grateful, Lord, that You always keep Your promises. Thank You that Your love never shakes.

GOD'S LOVE

Love is patient, love is kind. It does not envy, it does not boast, it is not proud. It does not dishonor others, it is not self-seeking, it is not easily angered, it keeps no record of wrongs. Love does not delight in evil but rejoices with the truth. It always protects, always trusts, always hopes, always perseveres. Love never fails.

1 CORINTHIANS 13:4–8 NIV

This is a familiar passage of scripture, one that's often read at weddings. We think of it as a mini-sermon on how we are to behave when we love someone. And it is that. But we can also apply these words to God. In fact, we could replace the word "love" with the word "God": God is patient, God is kind. God does not envy, God does not boast, God is not proud. God does not dishonor you, He is not self-seeking, He is not easily angered, He keeps no record of wrongs. God does not delight in evil but rejoices with the truth. God always protects, always trusts, always hopes, always perseveres. God never fails.

Oh God, I'm so grateful for Your kindness, Your patience, Your protection. Thank You for showing me how true love acts.

PRAISE

My lips will glorify You because Your faithful love is better than life.
PSALM 63:3 HCSB

The word translated "glorify" here means the same thing as "to praise." It's a little like the feeling you might have if a child you love does something amazing, and you can't help but smile and say how proud you feel. It's also a little like looking at the person you love and feeling your heart spill over, simply because you love to be in that person's presence. Or you could say it's like the long "ohhhh" that people often utter when they're astounded by something overwhelmingly beautiful. It's that urge to vocalize our feelings of love, pride, gratitude, and awe.

Praising God is just a natural part of the love relationship we have with Him. We don't do it because He's selfish and egotistical and needs to be constantly reassured that we love Him. We do it because it simply pours out of us. God's love is the best thing we will ever experience. It's better than life itself. No wonder we praise Him!

God, my lips can't help but speak Your praise;
my heart can't keep from singing of Your glory.
Your love fills me up—and then it just spills out of me.

IT'S UP TO YOU

Keep yourselves in the love of God.

JUDE 1:21 KJV

God's love is everywhere. He never holds it back. Nothing can separate you from it. And yet you can choose to put yourself where you can no longer experience it.

That doesn't mean His love isn't as real and present as ever. But if you allow anything to block your vision of God, whether it's a person, a thing, or an occupation, you'll no longer be able to perceive what's right there with you. The Bible calls it "hardening your heart." As you let other things become more important to you than God, your heart is no longer sensitive to God's presence. Your spiritual senses become dulled.

But why would you choose to live like that? God's love is always there, freely available, and God is always waiting, patiently and lovingly, for you to turn back to Him. Life goes so much better, has so much more joy and peace in it, when we're walking hand in hand with God.

God, when I can no longer feel Your love, remind me not to blame You. Instead, help me to remember to check my own heart and mind. I don't want anything to be more important to me than You are.

PATIENT LOVE

May the Lord lead your hearts into a full understanding and expression of the love of God and the patient endurance that comes from Christ.
2 THESSALONIANS 3:5 NLT

The Bible tells you over and over that God loves you. And yet you still may not be able to grasp the reality. And that's okay. God understands. Our human brains are incapable of understanding love that is totally unconditional, utterly limitless, eternal, and permanent. That's why the apostle Paul, who wrote this verse, prayed that the Lord might lead us into a full understanding—because Paul knew we would need God's help. We can't love like God loves without God's assistance. We can't even understand His love without His aid.

This understanding doesn't come to us quickly. It will take a lifetime of living with God to begin to really comprehend His love. It may even take an eternity. But that's okay too. Because Christ is patient—and He will help you to be patient too.

Dear Christ Jesus, You know I can't comprehend Your love. My mind is just too small to grasp all that Your love means. Thank You that You're willing to teach me. I'm ready to learn.

LOVE IN HUMAN FORM

When the kindness and love of God our Savior appeared, he saved us, not because of righteous things we had done, but because of his mercy. He saved us through the washing of rebirth and renewal by the Holy Spirit, whom he poured out on us generously through Jesus Christ our Savior, so that, having been justified by his grace, we might become heirs having the hope of eternal life. This is a trustworthy saying. And I want you to stress these things, so that those who have trusted in God may be careful to devote themselves to doing what is good.

TITUS 3:4–8 NIV

The kindness and love of God are wrapped up in Jesus. He is God's love in human form. Each thing He did was an expression of God's love. Nothing He did was because of anything we did to prove ourselves worthy. You don't have to earn God's love. And you don't have to earn Jesus.

Jesus is the incarnation of God's mercy, generosity, and grace. He shows you what God's love looks like. And in return, you can show Him your love by devoting your life to doing good—to imitating the behavior of Jesus when He was here on earth.

Jesus, I am so grateful that You came to show me the love of God. Thank You for Your mercy, Your kindness. Thank You for the renewal You give to me so generously. I want to do whatever I can to show You my love in return.

THE HOLY SPIRIT

This hope will not lead to disappointment.
For we know how dearly God loves us, because he has
given us the Holy Spirit to fill our hearts with his love.
Romans 5:5 NLT

People disappoint each other. Even the best, most loving people eventually do something to hurt the ones they love. But God's love will never disappoint you. You can trust Him.

If you have a hard time believing that this is true, ask the Holy Spirit to help you. That's why the Bible refers to the Spirit as the helper, the one who comes alongside us and keeps us company, even when we're at our weakest—the one who enters into our hearts and makes a home there. The Spirit is the one who can fill your heart with God's love. When you feel as though you are losing hope, when it doesn't seem possible that God really loves you, the Spirit is a reliable helper who always longs to reveal to you how dearly God loves you.

Spirit, I need Your help. Without You, I can't always believe that God could possibly love me. Please fill my heart. Help me to experience God's love in such a way that all my doubts are erased.

A HEALTHY TREE

I am like a flourishing olive tree in the house of God;
I trust in God's faithful love forever and ever.
PSALM 52:8 HCSB

God's faithful love is what you need to be spiritually healthy. With God's love, you have everything you need to grow. You won't just survive; you'll flourish. A healthy olive tree bears fruit—and so will you.

This doesn't mean you'll walk around with a perpetual smile on your face while you spout Bible verses. What it does mean is that God's love will spill out from you into the world in practical, concrete ways, ways that make the world a better place. When you're firmly rooted in God's love, you'll be able to branch out, bringing peace, justice, and compassion to the world around you. The more love you receive from God, the more love you'll have to give others.

It's a process that will never end. As your love affair with God continues forever and ever, so too will you continue to eternally bear fruit in God's house.

Thank You, Lord, for Your faithful love that never ends.
Thank You that because of You, I can grow and flourish.
Like a healthy tree, may I sink my roots deep into You, and may
my branches reach out wide, filled with fruit to feed the world.

IDOLS

"Those who cling to worthless idols turn away from God's love for them."
JONAH 2:8 NIV

An idol is anything that takes God's place in our lives. It could be a car or a house. It might be an activity, such as shopping or watching television or looking at Facebook. It could be a person or a professional role. It might be acquiring money or being popular or feeling important.

None of these things in and of themselves are bad things. God delights to give us His blessings. But if we let those blessings become more important to us than God is, then we turn away from God's love. We ignore the one who created us and loves us.

God doesn't stop loving us. He never will, and He never could. But we can choose to focus on other things. We think those things will make us happy—but without God, everything is empty and meaningless.

Don't cling to worthless things. Let them go—and turn back to the God who loves you.

Forgive me, I pray, dear Lord, for the times when I've chosen to give my attention to anything besides You. Please get my attention when You see me starting to stray from Your side. I want You with me. I want to share my entire life with You.

LIKE GOD

Whenever, though, they turn to face God as Moses did, God removes the veil and there they are—face-to-face! They suddenly recognize that God is a living, personal presence, not a piece of chiseled stone. And when God is personally present, a living Spirit, that old, constricting legislation is recognized as obsolete. We're free of it! All of us! Nothing between us and God, our faces shining with the brightness of his face. And so we are transfigured much like the Messiah, our lives gradually becoming brighter and more beautiful as God enters our lives and we become like him.

2 CORINTHIANS 3:16–18 MSG

Human beings have a tendency to get mixed up. We give our love and attention to the creation instead of to the Creator who made everything. But God's love is patient and forgiving. Again and again, He pulls our attention back to Him. And then we realize all over again—God is *real*. He is alive, and He is the only one who gives life to everything in the world. Suddenly, everything looks different. We realize that God offers us not only love but also freedom, light, and joy. He wants to make us like Him!

When I start to connect You with a lifeless religion that wants to tell me what I can't do, bring me back face-to-face with Your living presence. Fill me with Your light. Make me like You.

GOD'S WORD

Whoever keeps His word, truly in him the love of God is perfected. This is how we know we are in Him.

1 JOHN 2:5 HCSB

What exactly was John talking about here? If we break it down into the literal meanings of the original Greek words, we can understand a little better what John is trying to tell us. When he wrote that we are to "keep God's word," the Greek that is translated "keep" means to "watch over, to guard." The Greek used in the original for "word" means "speech, thought, or idea." In other words, in order for God's love to come to perfection—or reach its fullness—in you, you need to guard God's thoughts within you. You need to read His Word, the Bible, and you need to pay attention to how Jesus lived His life. And you need to be constantly meditating on God's thoughts—until they become your thoughts. When that happens, God's love has room to stretch out and grow. It can reach toward its perfect expression within you.

When I struggle to understand Your Word, God, I ask that Your Spirit will give me clarity. Show me how to guard Your thoughts, how to dwell on them daily, keeping close track of them. Let me not forget You, Lord. I want Your love to grow and develop inside me.

GOD LIVES IN US

No one has ever seen God. But if we love each other,
God lives in us, and his love is brought to full expression in us.
1 JOHN 4:12 NLT

Is it really possible to have a love relationship with someone you can't see? Someone you can't touch with your hands or hear with your ears? How do you know you're not just imagining things?

First of all, it's okay to use your imagination to picture God's presence in your life. You might imagine Jesus walking at your side—or you could picture God's hands holding all your troubles. Used properly, your imagination can be a powerful spiritual tool. Ask the Holy Spirit to help you keep your imagination on track, in line with God's thinking.

Second, the way we grow in God's love is by loving other people, the ones we *can* see. This doesn't mean we'll necessarily feel fond of everyone—but we can practice acting in love, demonstrating kindness and compassion to everyone who crosses our path. As we do this, God lives in us. He works through us. His love has room to grow inside our hearts.

Show me, Lord, how to love the people in my life—even the people I don't like very much. Teach me practical ways of showing Your mercy to others. May I find ways to offer a helping hand, to reach out, to accept and never judge. Use me to be Your hands, Your voice, Your smile, Your touch.

RIGHTEOUSNESS

God's business is putting things right; he loves getting the lines straight, setting us straight. Once we're standing tall, we can look him straight in the eye.

PSALM 11:7 MSG

Did you know that the word *righteous* has to do with making things straight? We think of someone who's righteous as being a moral person, a good person. But the ancient, literal meaning of the word is what's used in this translation: straight lines.

A straight line is the shortest distance between two points, and that's what God loves to do—He makes a straight path from His heart to ours. We can choose to wander around and take the long way, but we don't have to. God has marked our path for us, and He delights in showing us the way.

And then when we come close to Him, we can stand up straight, in our full stature, and look God right in the eye. Can you imagine? You and God eye to eye, His gaze telling you how much He loves you.

Thank You, Lord, that You have drawn a straight path for me to follow. Give me eyes to see Your way, and give me strength to follow it. I don't want to waste my time wandering off into the weeds. I want to reach Your presence as quickly as I can. I want to look You straight in the eye.

SEEK

Watch this: God's eye is on those who respect him, the ones who are looking for his love. He's ready to come to their rescue in bad times; in lean times he keeps body and soul together.

PSALM 33:18–19 MSG

God loves us all the time, no matter what. But He doesn't usually knock us over the head to get our attention, nor does He shout in our ears. Sometimes God *does* go to drastic lengths to reach us. Think about Saul on the road to Damascus. Saul had gotten so far off track, all the while thinking he was serving God, that Jesus appeared to him in a flash of light so bright that Saul was blinded. But that was a pretty unusual circumstance. Most of the time, we have to look for God's love.

Jesus promised us that the person who seeks will find (Matthew 7:7). God doesn't play hide-and-seek with us. If you look for God's love, you're guaranteed to find it.

Thank You, Jesus, for all Your promises. Thank You for helping me to understand more clearly how much You love me. When I feel as though God has abandoned me, when I doubt that God really loves me, remind me that all I have to do is seek—and You've promised me that I'll find what I'm looking for. I just have to ask, and You'll show me Your love.

NOTHING GETS LOST

God's love is meteoric, his loyalty astronomic, his purpose titanic, his verdicts oceanic. Yet in his largeness nothing gets lost; not a man, not a mouse, slips through the cracks.

Psalm 36:5–6 MSG

God's love is enormous, brilliant, deep—like a meteor, like the stars, like the ocean. No matter how many words we use to describe His love, we'll always run out. We'll never be able to express all that God's love is and does.

But sometimes such immensity can be overwhelming. We feel as though we could be sucked into it and disappear, as though we might lose our sense of individuality in the great sea of God's love. Or we worry that we're so little that God might easily overlook us.

That isn't how God's love works, though. He never takes away our uniqueness. We don't get lost. Instead, we become the people God always meant us to be, our truest, best selves. And no matter how small we feel ourselves to be, in God's eyes we are beloved. He sees everything, even the tiniest subatomic particles, and He treasures each infinitesimal piece of His creation. Nothing gets lost.

Your love is too great for me to understand, Lord.
Thank You that I don't have to understand it to experience it.
Thank You that You see me, You treasure me, and You are helping me to become exactly the person You created me to be.

STRESS

Because of the Lord's great love we are not consumed, for his compassions never fail.
Lamentations 3:22 NIV

Sometimes it feels as though life eats us up. So many crazy things are going on in the world at large that we wonder if we're safe; we worry about the people we love. Our responsibilities—work, family, finances, relationships, community—can be so stressful. By the end of each day, we're often exhausted, and we don't always wake up the next morning feeling very refreshed. Stress and tension are literally consuming our bodies, our minds, and our spirits, eating away at our health and our peace of mind.

But it doesn't have to be like that. God's love for you is so great that He wants to carry your stress for you. He longs for you to give it to Him so that He can replace it with His peace. It hurts Him to see you suffering needlessly when He's right there by your side, waiting to help you.

Dearest Lord, You know what my life is like. I don't have to tell You, because You already know everything about me. You know how tired I am, how stressed I feel. Thank You that You have compassion for me. Thank You that Your love for me will never fail.

TRAPPED

"I will say to the prisoners, 'Come out in freedom,' and to those in darkness, 'Come into the light.' They will be my sheep, grazing in green pastures and on hills that were previously bare. They will neither hunger nor thirst. The searing sun will not reach them anymore. For the LORD in his mercy will lead them; he will lead them beside cool waters. And I will make my mountains into level paths for them. . . . See, my people will return from far away."

ISAIAH 49:9–12 NLT

Do you ever feel as though you're trapped in some dark place? No matter how hard you try to get out, the walls always close in around you again. It could be almost anything in life that makes you feel that way. Your emotions. A bad habit. A hurtful relationship. An unrewarding job. A physical condition. It doesn't matter what it is—God wants to set you free. He wants to lead you into freedom, into a cool, green place where you can be nourished and restored. Turn to Him. He'll show you the way.

Shepherd of my soul, I am so grateful that You understand me, even when I feel like I'm far away. I'm glad Your love can reach me no matter how trapped I feel. Please show me the path that leads through this situation to You.

MOTHER-LOVE

"Can a mother forget her nursing child? Can she feel no love for the child she has borne? But even if that were possible, I would not forget you!"
ISAIAH 49:15 NLT

These verses give us another image of God's love. A nursing mother is incapable of forgetting her baby for long. Her own body will remind her before too much time goes by. Most mothers love their children with a love like no other, the sort of love that gets up in the middle of the night when she hears her child's cry, the sort of love that would make her even lay down her life without a thought. And that's the way God loves *you*. He loves you with a mother's love. You are woven into the very fiber of His being. He always hears your cry. He's incapable of ignoring you.

God, when I read what the Bible says about Your love, it's hard to believe You can really feel so strongly about me. As I spend time with You each day, help me to gain more confidence in the reality of Your love.

HOLDING GOD'S HAND

"I have chosen you and will not throw you away.
Don't be afraid, for I am with you. Don't be discouraged,
for I am your God. I will strengthen you and help you.
I will hold you up with my victorious right hand."
ISAIAH 41:9–10 NLT

Do you ever feel as though you'd like to throw yourself away? You get so sick of making the same mistakes over and over. You feel embarrassed that others can see your failures, and that hateful little voice inside you keeps saying that you're not good enough, that you'll never measure up, that you might as well just give up and stop trying.

God's heart aches when those feelings overtake you. He longs to take them away. He wants to assure you that He will never, ever throw you away. "Don't be discouraged," He's whispering to you. "I chose you and I love you so much. Let Me help you. I can make you stronger. I can give you victory over all the things you think are holding you back. Hold My hand."

Oh God, thank You for loving me.
Sometimes I just don't know what else to say but that!

LONG-DISTANCE LOVE

The Lord appeared to him long ago, saying, "I have loved you with an everlasting love; therefore I have drawn you out with kindness."

JEREMIAH 31:3 NASB

We need to draw close to God in order to truly feel His love. But that doesn't mean He's not still pursuing us, even while we feel as though we're far away. This verse says that the Lord appeared to Jeremiah from long ago, crossing the time and space between them with a message of love. Even when you're running in the opposite direction, God's love is like a gentle tractor beam, pulling you back to Him. It can even come to you from the past.

Look back at your childhood. Can you see that God was sprinkling His love into your memories? God's love knows no time. He has loved you since before you were born; He loved you all through your childhood and adolescence, through all the years of your adulthood; and He will love you for eternity.

Thank You, loving Lord, for loving me even when I turn away from You. Thank You for loving me from afar, and thank You for loving me even through my memories. Draw me closer to You. I don't want there to be any distance between us any longer.

RESTORED

"I will build you again and you will be rebuilt, virgin of Israel! You will take up your tambourines again, and go out to the dances of the revelers."

JEREMIAH 31:4 NASB

God's love can transform you into an innocent, happy child again. No, you can't go backward in time, and nothing can undo what's been done in the physical world. And yet through the love of God, you can be rebuilt. You'll be intact and whole again, no matter how many ways you've been broken in the past.

Like Jesus, you may bear the scars of the past. But they'll no longer be bleeding wounds. They'll become reminders of God's immense love for you, a love that heals and restores and makes all things new—even broken hearts.

Dearest Lord, I ask for Your healing touch on my heart. You know all the ways I've been wounded, all the ways my heart has felt violated. I know You have the power and love to mend everything in me that's broken. I open my heart to You, trusting You to bring wholeness and innocence to everything in me that feels soiled and used. Give me a child's heart once more—and I'll shake my tambourine and dance with joy!

CHRIST'S HOME

Christ will make his home in your hearts as you trust in him. Your roots will grow down into God's love and keep you strong. And may you have the power to understand, as all God's people should, how wide, how long, how high, and how deep his love is.

EPHESIANS 3:17–18 NLT

You don't have to go searching for God's presence. Maybe it's easier to feel Him with you when you're in church, or maybe you sense God most when you're somewhere beautiful in nature. But really, Christ's home is inside your very own heart. That means He is with you no matter where you go. And the more you trust Him, the more you'll feel Him there inside you. It's one of those happy cycles (the opposite of a vicious one): the more you feel Christ in you, the more you'll trust Him; and the more you trust Him, the more you'll feel Him in you. And as this cycle turns around and around, your roots will be growing more deeply and more firmly into God's love. You'll begin to understand the greatest mystery of all—how wide and long, how high and deep God's love truly is.

I am so glad, Lord Jesus, that You feel comfortable making Your home within my heart. Help me to trust You more. I want to be rooted deep in Your love.

GOD'S SONG

When my soul is in the dumps, I rehearse everything I know of you. . . . Then God *promises to love me all day, sing songs all through the night! My life is God's prayer.*

Psalm 42:6, 8 msg

We all have times when we feel down in the dumps. But instead of wallowing in sadness and discouragement, you can use those times to think extra hard about God. Go over in your mind everything you know about His love. Read the Bible, paying special attention to all the verses that speak of the ways God loves you. Remember things He's done for you in the past. Spend time in prayer.

And before long, instead of singing the blues, you'll find yourself singing a duet with God. He will love you all through the hardest days, and He'll sing you lullabies as you fall asleep. Your entire life will be a song of prayer.

God, when my soul is in the dumps, remind me to think of You. Instead of dwelling on everything that's wrong in my life, may I remember all the wonderful things You have done for me. Teach me to turn to You whenever sadness hits my heart. I don't want to hear that little voice inside me that speaks only gloom and doom. I'll listen instead to Your love songs.

COMPLETE

May you experience the love of Christ, though it is too great to understand fully. Then you will be made complete with all the fullness of life and power that comes from God.

EPHESIANS 3:19 NLT

Sometimes we feel as though we go through life with a few pieces missing. Maybe we feel as though we never had the full set of pieces we needed—or maybe we sense we've lost a few in the onslaught of life's challenges and frustrations. Either way, that feeling leads to a lack of self-worth.

But Christ wants to take away any self-doubts we have. As we experience more and more of His love, we will grow into the complete and whole versions of ourselves that God always had in mind for us. We will be filled up with God's life and power—until absolutely nothing is missing.

Lord Jesus, I know I can never fully understand the love You have for me, but I want to experience more and more of it. I know that as I rest in Your love, soaking it up, I will become whole. I'll become everything God created me to be, filled with Your strength, Your endless life. Only in You can I become the me I've always most wanted to be.

BROKENHEARTED

He heals the brokenhearted and binds up their wounds.
PSALM 147:3 NIV

Sometimes life breaks our hearts. It doesn't matter how many blessings we've been given or how many privileges we enjoy—sooner or later, something comes along that wounds us to the core. Heartbreak can feel like a physical wound. In fact, researchers are finding that it can have many of the same dangers and complications that an actual physical injury would bring. Emotions affect your body, and the hurricane of pain and stress that follows heartbreak can do very real damage to your body.

Jesus understands those feelings. After all, when He was on earth, His heart was broken too; the Gospels tell us of times when He cried with sorrow. And when your heart breaks, His heart is breaking right along with it. He is with you in the midst of the pain.

God is always close to those who are hurt and in need of healing, and He doesn't leave anyone to suffer their pain alone. Instead, He stays near to help guide those who are hurting so that they can find healing. Jesus can mend broken hearts just as surely as He made blind eyes see and straightened disabled limbs while He was on earth.

Thank You, Jesus, that You understand my aching heart. I ask You to heal me.

SAVED BY GRACE

But God, who is rich in mercy, because of His great love that He had for us, made us alive with the Messiah even though we were dead in trespasses. You are saved by grace!

EPHESIANS 2:4–5 HCSB

The literal meaning of the Greek word our Bibles translate as "grace" is kindness. It contains within its meaning the image of someone stretching out their arms, freely extending themselves toward someone in need of their help. It is something that by its very nature gives joy and pleasure. It brings freedom. It is love in action.

God's graciousness is a permanent part of His nature. We don't have to do anything to earn His grace or wait until He is in a good mood. Graciousness is not something He takes off and puts on, depending on the circumstances. It's just who He is. He demonstrates grace in everything He does.

I know You are on my side, Lord. You want me to be whole. You want me to trust You so that I can receive Your blessings. You want to give me the capacity to walk in Your grace and wrap myself in Your love. You are the Creator of the world, and I know nothing is too hard for You—Your grace is all I need to live.

PRECIOUS, HONORED, LOVED

You are precious to me. You are honored, and I love you.
Isaiah 43:4 NLT

The speaker here is God. And this is what He says to you: "I value you. You are important to Me. You are precious to Me. When I look at you, I see someone who is utterly beautiful." Then He adds, "I respect you. I hold you in esteem. I honor you. I defend your dignity. I want to guard you from all injuries to your heart and spirit." Finally, He says to you, "I love you!"

That is how the Creator of the universe feels about you! It's hard to comprehend—but it's true.

Dear God, You have given me so much love. Help me in return to love You more and more. Let my heart always seek You first; teach me not to expect anyone or anything to give me what only You can give. I want to depend more and more on Your grace; I want to believe more and more in Your love; I want to rely more and more on Your promises. Fill me with Your Spirit, I pray. Make me more able to receive Your love. And may I grow more capable of returning Your love.

COVENANT LOVE

Know therefore that the Lord your God is God; he is the faithful God, keeping his covenant of love to a thousand generations.
DEUTERONOMY 7:9 NIV

A covenant is an unbreakable promise between two people. God's love covenant promises us an eternity of life—and in return, He asks us to put everything we have and are in His hands. This act of total trust would be impossible if we thought God might drop the things we give Him—or if we suspected He might actually wish to harm us and make us unhappy. But God's love is like no human being's. It wants only our good; there is nothing selfish in it.

A covenant is reciprocal. It works from both directions. When God asks us to trust Him with our entire lives, He has already given us Himself—totally, endlessly, both through Jesus and through the Spirit. We can relax in His love, knowing we are completely safe and secure. We give Him our whole selves, knowing His love will never diminish us or shame us or hurt us. Through Jesus and the Holy Spirit, we can enter a new relationship with God, one that's built on a covenant of absolutely unconditional love.

Dear God, I may never be able to truly grasp how much You love me—but I thank You anyway. Thank You for sending Your Son into the world. Thank You that through Him, I can experience the life of Your Spirit. Thank You for Your covenant of love that reaches further into the future than I can even see.

THE GOOD SHEPHERD

"I am the good shepherd; the good shepherd lays down His life for the sheep."
JOHN 10:11 NASB

A shepherd walks among his sheep. He never goes off to pursue his own business. The sheep *are* his business. He constantly makes sure they have all that they need.

So when Jesus says that He is the shepherd, He means you are His sheep. You can rest in the knowledge that He will meet your needs. He will lead you down paths in life that lead to health and happiness. Even better, His paths will lead more deeply into His divine nature, which will be to you a source of life, strengthening and restoring you whenever you are weak or wounded.

Even when you wander off His paths (and we all make mistakes), Jesus will follow after you, and He'll never stop searching for you until you are safe once more with Him. When you can't find the strength to take another step, He will lift you up and carry you in His arms. Each thing He does shows you His love, for He is always leading you to a place of blessing, a place of nourishing green grass.

Dear Jesus, thank You for being my shepherd. I am so grateful for all the care and attention You give me. Help me to follow You even more closely.

LONELY

Heart-shattered lives ready for love don't for a moment escape God's notice. Make Zion the place you delight in, repair Jerusalem's broken-down walls.
Psalm 51:17–18 MSG

Do you ever feel invisible? Everyone around you is so busy with their own problems and preoccupations. You don't want to be self-centered, and you don't want to exaggerate your troubles, but sometimes you feel so lonely. You wonder if you ran down the street naked, shouting at the top of your lungs, would anyone even notice?

God always notices. You don't have to jump up and down and scream to get His attention. His heart is always turned toward you; His ear is always listening for your cry. He's like a loving mother whose eye is always on her toddler, always anticipating danger, always quick to swoop in and comfort with hugs and kisses.

So when your heart is shattered, when you're lonely and longing for love, turn to the one who is always there. He is waiting to bless and comfort you. He wants to build you up, healing everything that is broken in you. He loves you so much. He delights in your presence!

When my heart is hurting and I feel lonely and forgotten, remind me, loving Lord, to turn to You. Repair my broken walls. And I will delight in Your presence, just as You delight in mine.

HUMILITY AND WORRY

So humble yourselves under the mighty power of God, and at the right time he will lift you up in honor. Give all your worries and cares to God, for he cares about you.

1 PETER 5:6–7 NLT

It takes humility to let go of our worries. As much as we think we *hate* the anxiety that keeps us awake at night and makes our stomachs churn, we hold on to it. We cling to those worries as though we love them, letting them occupy our minds until there's little room for anything else.

God cares about you. He longs to relieve you of your worries. But He can't do that until you release them into His hand. That means you have to let go of your own control. You have to admit there is nothing you can do to get rid of your anxiety—except give it to God. And then you'll have to trust Him to deal with the outcomes of all those situations that are making you fret. When you let go of your demand that things turn out the way *you* want them to, you can finally relax into God's love, trusting Him to deal with everything in His time, in His way.

It's so hard, God, to let go of my worries. I feel as though by thinking about them constantly, I somehow have more control over them. But I know that's not true—so I'm giving them to You. And when I take them back—as I know I will—remind me all over again to put them back in Your loving hands.

THE COMPASSION OF THE LORD

Just as a father has compassion on his children,
so the LORD has compassion on those who fear Him.
PSALM 103:13 NASB

Letting go of our lives doesn't come easily. As much as we may want to surrender everything to God, somehow a part of us insists on holding on.

As a result, sometimes we may feel as though God is withholding His love from us as a punishment for our lack of surrender to His will. That's not the way God works though. The natural consequence of holding on to our lives, refusing to give them to God, is that we trip over our own feet. We prevent ourselves from being as effective and productive and creative as God longs for us to be. We shut ourselves off from the many ways that God longs to demonstrate His love to us and through us. But none of those are punishments from God. They're all things we do to ourselves.

Meanwhile, God understands our human nature (after all, He created us!), and He knows how hard it is for us to surrender to Him. God has compassion, the way a good parent has compassion, and He is patient with our weakness. He knows that surrender is a lifelong process that can't be accomplished by sheer willpower. He knows we can't do anything without His help.

Thank You, Lord, for Your unending compassion.

LEARNING FROM JESUS

"Come to me, all of you who are weary and carry heavy burdens, and I will give you rest. Take my yoke upon you. Let me teach you, because I am humble and gentle at heart, and you will find rest for your souls."
MATTHEW 11:28–29 NLT

No matter how many times we doubt God, He never judges us for our lack of faith. He is patient and gentle with us. He gives us time to learn just how much He really loves us. He doesn't expect us to know or understand His love without His help. We just have to let Him teach us.

Some of us are slower learners than others. We resist God's teaching. Instead of trusting God, we "lean on our own understanding" (see Proverbs 3:5). We're stubborn. And yet God still patiently holds out His love to us. "Let Me teach you," whispers Jesus in our ears. "Please. You'd experience so much more peace if you would." But there we go, still struggling along in our own strength, growing more and more weary and anxious and downhearted. "I can teach you how to rest," Jesus murmurs. "Let Me show you."

It's a long, slow process. We make things harder for ourselves. Sadly, some of us will probably never fully enter the rest Jesus longs for us to experience until after we die. That's our choice. Jesus' gentle love is still held out.

You don't have to wait! You can begin right now to learn about God's love.

Thank You, Jesus, for being willing to teach me about Your love.

KNOWN BY GOD

You have searched me, Lord, and you know me. You know when I sit and when I rise; you perceive my thoughts from afar. You discern my going out and my lying down; you are familiar with all my ways.

Psalm 139:1–3 NIV

This passage is a powerful statement of God's love for you. He knows you through and through. He knows when you get up and when you sit down. Even if you've turned away from God, even if God is the furthest thing from your thoughts, He knows your thoughts. He sees everywhere you go during the day, and He knows when you go to bed. He understands what motivates your actions. Everything about you is familiar to Him. Why? Because His love for you occupies every moment of His being. There is never an instant when He is not paying attention to you. He knows your ins and outs, your quirks, your warts, your hidden beauty, your dreams and fears. He notes the smallest details of your days. There is nothing too small about you or your life for Him to care about.

Lord, thank You for Your immense care for me.
I am so grateful that You know me so well, and You love me anyway.

SURROUNDED

You go before me and follow me.
You place your hand of blessing on my head.
PSALM 139:5 NLT

This verse expresses David's total confidence in God's love. The idea of going before and after comes from the Hebrew word *tsuwr*, which was often used to describe a military fort, a place that was totally enclosed and safe. Like a castle surrounded by fortifications and a deep moat, God's love protects you from all dangers. Nothing can reach you without passing through His love. God guards you on all sides, past, present, and future.

You may feel weak sometimes—we all do—but feelings are not always accurate when it comes to the truth of God's love. He is always with you to keep you and strengthen you. In the spiritual realm, you are completely safe. God's hand of blessing rests always on your head. You are surrounded by love.

Lord, when I doubt Your love, remind me that You constantly surround me. Teach me to see from Your perspective; help me to live more and more in the spiritual realm, so that the reality there shines forth on my physical life, transforming everything that happens to me into an expression of Your love. I want to see Your hand at work in my life, blessing everything it touches.

EVERYWHERE

Where can I go from Your Spirit? Or where can I flee from Your presence? If I ascend to heaven, You are there; if I make my bed in Sheol, behold, You are there. If I take up the wings of the dawn, if I dwell in the remotest part of the sea, even there Your hand will lead me, and Your right hand will take hold of me.

PSALM 139:7–10 NASB

Benson's Bible commentary has this to say about these verses: "If I were able, with the swiftness of the rays of the rising sun, in an instant to shoot myself to the remotest parts of the earth or sea, even there should thy hand lead me—I should still exist in thee: thy presence would be diffused all around me; and thine enlivening power would support my frame."

Dear Lord, I can go nowhere where Your love is not. Your love is everywhere. Even if I were to travel to outer space, even if I were to go down into the realm of the dead, Your love would still be there. Your presence has no boundaries; it goes everywhere, even into the darkness of pain and sin. Thank You that nothing has the power to divide me from Your love.

STEADFAST LOVE

God makes everything come out right; he puts victims back on their feet. . . . God is sheer mercy and grace; not easily angered, he's rich in love. He doesn't endlessly nag and scold, nor hold grudges forever. He doesn't treat us as our sins deserve, nor pay us back in full for our wrongs. As high as heaven is over the earth, so strong is his love to those who fear him. And as far as sunrise is from sunset, he has separated us from our sins. As parents feel for their children, God feels for those who fear him. He knows us inside and out.

Psalm 103:6, 8–14 MSG

These verses repeatedly use the Hebrew word *hesed*, which is translated as "love." *Hesed*, however, is a particular kind of love. It is steadfast. Nothing changes it; it has no end.

This love is also a forgiving love. Not even your failures and flaws can diminish it. It is the sort of love that good parents have for their children, the sort of love that automatically and instantly forgives, that seeks always to heal and lift up. And it's a love that is as high as the sky, as wide as the horizon. It separates you from your sin—everything that might come between you and God—and fills the space with love.

God knows the best version of you—the you He created you to be—and His steadfast love will never stop working to create the beloved person who is *you*!

Thank You, Lord, for Your unending, unfailing, steadfast love.

NO MORE HIDING

If I say, "Surely the darkness will overwhelm me, and the light around me will be night," even darkness is not dark to You, and the night is as bright as the day. Darkness and light are alike to You.

Psalm 139:11–12 NASB

God knows you intimately. Today's verse is a wonderful declaration of God's love—but it can also feel a little uncomfortable. After all, we all hide pieces of ourselves, even from those people we love and trust the most. We even hide pieces of ourselves from our own selves. But we have no hope of pushing the unwelcome aspects of ourselves into the shadows where God won't see them. He sees in the dark as easily as He does in the light, and nothing is hidden from Him.

God sees you better than you see yourself. And He still loves you! As you connect to that love, allowing it to fill you, you won't need to hide in the dark anymore.

You see me so clearly, Lord. Nothing within me is hidden from You. When that thought scares me, remind me, God of love, that everything about me is covered by Your love. There is nothing about me that You don't see—and Your love is so immense, so encompassing, that it wraps around every piece of me.

MADE WITH LOVE

You created my inmost being; you knit me together in my mother's womb. I praise you because I am fearfully and wonderfully made.

PSALM 139:13–14 NIV

Do you ever think about the fact that your body is itself a gift of God's love? Most of us tend to complain about our bodies. They're too fat, too short, too tall, too thin. Our society has taught us that there is only one kind of beauty—and since most of us fall short of that "perfection," we feel as though something is wrong with our bodies. We may wish God had given us an entirely different sort of beauty.

But no matter how fat or thin you are, no matter the shape of your thighs and belly, your body is "fearfully and wonderfully made." Even if you have certain limitations, there are still so many things your body's senses and muscles can do. Your heart keeps beating blood, your lungs keep breathing in oxygen and breathing out carbon dioxide, and your brain keeps thinking and learning. Your body is a gift of God's love!

Help me, loving Lord, to be more aware of all the blessings of my body—and to focus less on all its imperfections. Remind me that I have been knitted together with love.

ALWAYS IN HIS THOUGHTS

How precious are your thoughts about me,
O God. They cannot be numbered!
PSALM 139:17 NLT

Do you ever wonder if God can really be aware of you and your problems? After all, God has an entire world—an entire universe—to keep track of. How can He possibly give His attention to any single individual?

God is an infinite being. His ways are so far beyond ours that we can't even imagine them. He fills the entire world, and yet He is greater than the world. And this eternal, all-powerful, all-knowing, unlimited God loves you! You are constantly in His thoughts. There is never a moment of the day when He forgets you.

God, Your thoughts of me are so precious to me!
I don't understand how You can keep me in mind when I am
so small and You are so great—but I'm grateful You do.

TOO MANY TO COUNT

O Lord my God, you have performed many wonders for us. Your plans for us are too numerous to list. You have no equal. If I tried to recite all your wonderful deeds, I would never come to the end of them.

Psalm 40:5 NLT

The next time you're discouraged with yourself, with your life, or with the world in general, try doing this: make a list, starting with your earliest memories, of all the things God has done in your life. Don't overlook the smallest things; list them all, one after another.

If you keep going, a list like this could fill page after page. After a while, though, you'll probably get the picture. God's love has been at work in your life over the years in countless ways.

The psalmist came to this same realization. And then he realized that God's love also reaches into the future. Just as God has blessed you in the past, so He also has plans to bless you in the future. His plans for your future are as countless as the things He has already done in your life. He loves you that much!

*Thank You, God, for all You've done in my life—
and thank You for all You're going to do.*

IT'S MUTUAL

We love because he first loved us.
1 JOHN 4:19 NIV

A love relationship is mutual. God loves you—and in return, you just naturally come to love Him more and more.

Does God deserve your love? Well, what more could He do to earn your love than to give Himself to you? And He does give Himself, daily, moment by moment. And since He is God, what better gift could He offer than Himself?

So if you are looking for reasons to love God, here they are: God gives Himself to you—and He loved you first, even before you were born.

Loving Lord, I am so grateful for Your love. As You give Yourself to me, help me learn to love You more and more. Thank You for loving me my whole life long, even before I was conceived and for all eternity.

SET FREE

He led you out of your dark, dark cell, broke open the jail and led you out. So thank God for his marvelous love, for his miracle mercy to the children he loves; he shattered the heavy jailhouse doors, he snapped the prison bars like matchsticks!

Psalm 107:14–16 MSG

Most of us may never experience how it feels to be actually imprisoned—but we don't have to be behind actual bars to experience the feeling of being trapped in a prison cell. Prisons come in many shapes, from addiction to loneliness, and from lack of self-confidence to resentment. These emotional and psychological prisons can keep us from experiencing the life of love and joy that God wants us to have.

But there's good news. God's love has the power to shatter jailhouse doors. His light can shine into even the darkest prison cells. For some people, this may happen all at once, but for most of us it's a gradual process. Little by little, God's love knocks down our prison walls—and one day we realize we've been set free.

Dear Lord, set me free. I don't want to live within a prison cell any longer.

DEPENDING ON THE SHEPHERD

The Lord is my shepherd; I have all that I need.
Psalm 23:1 NLT

Sometimes we act as though God is the sheep and we are the shepherd. We seem to think that God will run away from us if we don't keep a close eye on Him. If we turn our backs even for a moment, He'll be gone. But that's not the way it works. God is the shepherd who is constantly watching you and guarding you. No matter how many times you turn away, He is always right there, calling you back to His side—because He loves you that much.

And yet often we don't truly believe that God is a good shepherd who will care for our needs. We expect Him to disappear when hard times come. We don't turn to Him for comfort and nourishment when our souls are starving, crying out in pain and hunger. We try to figure things out for ourselves instead of relying on the wisdom and strength of the shepherd.

Don't be afraid to depend on the shepherd of your soul. You don't have to understand everything, and you don't have to be strong all the time. You have someone who loves you so much that He will care for you when you are weak and confused—and He'll lead you into green pastures where you can grow and be nurtured.

Thank You, Jesus, for being the shepherd of my soul. Teach me to rely on You.

THE LOVE GIFT OF YOUR IDENTITY

The purposes of a person's heart are deep waters,
but one who has insight draws them out.
PROVERBS 20:5 NIV

Self-awareness is essential to understanding God's love for you. After all, if you have a gift but don't even know you have it, it will do you little good—nor can you say "thank You" to the giver. It will sit there unopened in your heart. You won't be able to use the gift for your own good or the good of those around you.

But self-awareness must be combined with humility. You can't take credit for this gift. As the apostle Paul wrote, "What do you have that God hasn't given you? And if everything you have is from God, why boast as though it were not a gift?" (1 Corinthians 4:7 NLT).

There's nothing wrong with enjoying the gifts you've received from God or even taking pride in them. You'll find your truest, brightest identity through the acknowledgment of these gifts. Where you'll run into problems, though, is when you act as though these gifts are something you created on your own, as though they aren't in fact God's love gifts to you.

Thank You, Lord, for all the gifts that are encapsulated in my identity.

KNOWING CHRIST

I want to know Christ and experience the mighty power that raised him from the dead.
PHILIPPIANS 3:10 NLT

If you know Christ, you'll have a better understanding of God's love, because Christ is the incarnation of the love of God. And the better you get to know Him, the more you'll appreciate the love of God. As you see what Jesus did on the cross, giving His life in love, you'll be filled with wonder—and you'll want to give your life back to Him. As you become totally secure in His love, you'll be able to love Him more and more in return.

And on top of that, you'll have more love to give to others, because the people who are most loved are the ones who have the most love to offer. As the apostle Paul wrote in his letter to the Philippians: "I pray that your love will overflow more and more" (1:9 NLT).

Lord Jesus, help me get to know You better and better. May this be the goal at the center of my entire life.

HARD TIMES

You prepare a table before me in the presence of my enemies;
You anoint my head with oil; my cup overflows.
PSALM 23:5 HCSB

We often feel as though God loves us during the happy times of our lives. If we get a raise, if we are healed from some illness, or if our children and our elderly parents are all happy and healthy, it's easy to say, "Thank You, God, for loving me." The good things in our lives feel like the expression of God's love.

But in this verse, the psalmist indicates that God loves you even when enemies surround you. Even when you're struggling with a problem at work or at home, when you feel sick, when someone you love is in trouble, God's love for you is just as great. God loves to bless you, but He also allows hard times to enter your life—and He continues to bless you, even in the middle of suffering and worry and disappointment. In fact, those are the times when you need His love even more. And it's always there for you. In happy times and hard, God's love is always the same.

God, You know that when life seems hard, when everything seems to be going wrong, it's easy for me to feel like You don't love me. Remind me that Your love does not change with outer circumstances. Anoint my head with the oil of Your devotion, Lord; fill my cup with Your love.

REMAINING

Just as the Father has loved Me,
I also have loved you; remain in My love.
JOHN 15:9 NASB

Jesus gave surprisingly few commands during His time on earth, but this verse is one: He tells you to remain in His love. In other words, you are to make your home in the love of Jesus. You are to stay inside it, not straying away from it. You are to dwell there, living out your life within its shelter.

The reasons for doing so are twofold: because nothing else makes sense (why would you want to live anywhere else?), and because nothing else is as good for you (nowhere else can you experience the abundant life that Jesus offers you).

Think about what this verse means. Jesus loves you in the same way that the Father loved Him! When you think about who is doing the loving here, whom He is loving, and how much He loves, how can you help but love Him in return? As the psalmist said, "If you are really wise, you'll think this over—it's time you appreciated GOD's deep love" (Psalm 107:43 MSG).

Jesus, Your love just boggles my mind when I try to grab hold of it. All I know is this—I want to make my home in Your love.

INFINITE GIFTS

"Every good thing I have comes from you."
PSALM 16:2 NLT

Even the best humans have an element of selfishness in their love. But that's not the case with God. His love is that total selflessness that "does not demand its own way" (1 Corinthians 13:5 NLT). It gives itself away freely, without demanding anything in return. His gifts are countless—the food you eat, the air you breathe, the light that shines on you, all the things that are necessary for life. The beauty of the world. Friendships and family. Dignity and wisdom. Your body's health and strength. Meaningful work. Laughter.

The list could go on and on for pages. God—the Holy One, the Supreme Being, the all-powerful Creator—gives you infinite gifts because He loves you infinitely. He sets no limits on His love.

Remind me, Lord, that You are the great giver who delights in bestowing on me endless blessings. Make me more aware of Your gifts as I go through my day. I praise You for all the wonderful things that fill my life. Since You set no limits on Your love for me, help me not to limit my love for You either.

UNFAILING LOVE

For if, while we were God's enemies, we were reconciled to him through the death of his Son, how much more, having been reconciled, shall we be saved through his life!
ROMANS 5:10 NIV

We all have days when we doubt God's love. The world can be a difficult place, and some days the shadows seem deeper and more real than the light. Terrible things happen, both in the world at large and in our own personal worlds.

In times like that, remind yourself of this truth: God is the one who truly loves you, loves you unconditionally, and loved you even while you were estranged from Him, even when you thought of Him as an enemy. In the apostle Paul's letter to the Romans, he adds, "Since he did not spare even his own Son but gave him up for us all, won't he also give us everything else?" (8:32 NLT). God loves you so much that He gave His Son for you—so you can count on Him to handle all that life brings. Even in the dark times, God's love never fails. It has never failed you in the past, it won't today, and it never will in the future.

Thank You, God, for loving me even before I knew how to love You back. When I feel filled with doubts and worry, give me strength to believe in Your love. On those days when the world feels like a frightening place, help me to rest in You.

ROCK SOLID

If an army encamps against me, my heart will not fear; If war arises against me, in spite of this I am confident. . . . On the day of trouble He will conceal me in His tabernacle; in the secret place of His tent He will hide me; He will lift me up on a rock.

PSALM 27:3, 5 NASB

In today's world, you have plenty of reasons to be afraid. And yet in spite of everything that's happening, you can say with the psalmist, "I shall be confident." When trouble comes—and face it, it always does sooner or later—God will hide you away in the tabernacle of His love. His love will be a solid rock you can stand on, no matter how much the world's ground shakes around you.

Thank You, God, that You will keep me safe.
Thank You that Your love is rock solid.

A SANCTUARY OF LOVE

You are so handsome, my love, pleasing beyond words!
The soft grass is our bed; fragrant cedar branches are the beams
of our house, and pleasant smelling firs are the rafters.
SONG OF SOLOMON 1:16–17 NLT

God loves you more than any lover ever could. And you can be like a bride rejoicing in His love, knowing that it comes to you through Jesus, who shows you what God's love looks like. Your heart is a private room you share with God, a secret place where God delights to spend time with you. As you spend time there, praying and meditating on God's love, you decorate this intimate sanctuary with flowers and beautiful colors. Your own inner being becomes a hideaway where you can go when the world gets to be too much for you, a place to spend time alone with the lover of your soul.

Lord, thank You for turning my heart into a sanctuary of love.
Teach me to retreat there more often so that we can spend time together.

HUNGRY AND THIRSTY

Blessed are they which do hunger and thirst
after righteousness: for they shall be filled.
MATTHEW 5:6 KJV

When you seek God rather than your own satisfaction, you find that life has more joy than when you put your selfish urges first. It's a paradox. The more you long for the presence of the living God, the more you hunger for even more—and the more joy you experience.

This perspective doesn't match up with what we absorb from our society, though. Everywhere we turn, we're given the message that our happiness depends on the world around us. And as long as you hold that attitude, the thought of giving everything to God can seem pretty uncomfortable, even distasteful. Christ's concept of love—which requires self-sacrifice—can seem like too great a challenge to attempt. When you are hungry for earthly things, your taste buds no longer respond to God's grace.

But as you learn to depend on God's love instead of worldly satisfactions, you'll begin to rest in thoughts of God, even as you're always restless, longing for still more.

I'm hungry for You, God. I'm thirsty for
Your love. Fill me, I pray, with Your Spirit.

INCOMPLETE

Now we see things imperfectly, like puzzling reflections in a mirror, but then we will see everything with perfect clarity. All that I know now is partial and incomplete, but then I will know everything completely, just as God now knows me completely.

1 CORINTHIANS 13:12 NLT

Many things about God are puzzling. Even though you're learning more about God's love every day, you'll never reach the moment when you can say, "There. I've figured it all out. Now I understand!"

And yet even now, in this life when so much is hidden from us, you can rest in the absolute knowledge of one thing: God loves you. Even as you long for the day when you'll see God's splendor totally revealed, the day when your own identity will fully reflect back His glory, you can relax now in the thought of Christ's abundant kindness and love. As the psalmist sang, "You will show me the way of life, granting me the joy of your presence and the pleasures of living with you forever" (Psalm 16:11 NLT).

My knowledge of You is so incomplete, God. But I know You love me. Help me to grow in understanding and love.

FORGIVEN AND HEALED

Let all that I am praise the LORD; may I never forget the good things he does for me. He forgives all my sins and heals all my diseases.
PSALM 103:2–3 NLT

If you spend your time thinking about compassion so undeserved, generosity so free, kindness so unexpected, mercy so limitless, grace so amazing, then the natural result will be that your very identity will become rooted in God's love. Your selfish desires will no longer seem so appealing. You will be more and more consumed with love for the one who loved you first, the one who gives Himself totally to healing you and making you whole.

Root me in Your love, Lord. I want to spend my time thinking about You, dwelling in You, until my entire identity is wrapped up in You, forgiven and healed.

REDEEMED

O Israel, wait and watch for God*—with* God*'s arrival comes love, with* God*'s arrival comes generous redemption. No doubt about it—he'll redeem Israel, buy back Israel from captivity to sin.*

Psalm 130:7–8 MSG

When something is redeemed, it's "bought back." God redeems your soul from captivity to sin, but He also buys back the past. All the years you thought were wasted, somehow God turns them to good. He heals the wounds the past has left on your soul, and He turns those wounds into strengths. You'll still bear the scars, but now those old wounds have become gifts you can share with others. Old disappointments will no longer hurt the way they once did. Old guilt will be completely removed from your heart so that you no longer have to carry its weight.

And why does God do all that? Because He loves you so much. So wait for Him. His arrival will bring more and more love into your life as He redeems you and restores all that sin has robbed from you.

God, I'm waiting for Your arrival in my life. I know You are bringing me more love than I can imagine—so I'm waiting and watching for You, confident that You are always on Your way to me. You will never leave me alone, for You are constantly redeeming me, buying me back from the hold sin has had on my life.

POURED OUT

He poured out his life.
ISAIAH 53:12 NIV

This pouring out of His life is what the Bible mentions again and again about God's nature. Even the name of God in Hebrew—Yahweh—means "Life Giver," the "Giver of Existence." God's very nature, His total identity, is encapsulated in His giving of life, His own life, to you.

Our God is a generous and giving God. Verse after verse in the Bible tell of His blessings, His gifts, His love. How much clearer could it be? God not only loves you; He loves you with all His heart.

Thank You, Lord, for pouring out Your life into me.
Fill me to the top—heart, mind, and body.

JESUS UNDERSTANDS

We do not have a high priest who cannot sympathize with our weaknesses, but One who has been tempted in all things just as we are, yet without sin. Therefore let's approach the throne of grace with confidence, so that we may receive mercy and find grace for help at the time of our need.

Hebrews 4:15–16 nasb

When we're going through life's challenges, it's good to have a friend we can turn to, someone who understands how we feel. Something about having a special friend who "gets us" helps to ease our pain.

But sometimes not even our closest friends understand us—and there are times when their love just can't stretch far enough to cover us. That can be a terribly lonely feeling. But the good news is this: Jesus always understands. He is God, but He is also human. He knows what it's like to have a body that aches with tiredness or illness; He understands the loneliness of being abandoned by friends; He even understands what it's like to feel weak and tempted.

And His love is so great that it can handle any situation. He always understands you—and He always, always loves you.

Jesus, thank You for coming to earth and living with us. Thank You that You always understand, You never condemn me, and You never stop loving me.

FROM ETERNITY TO ETERNITY

"From eternity to eternity I am God. No one can snatch anyone out of my hand. No one can undo what I have done."
ISAIAH 43:13 NLT

God is not merely the generous giver of life who provides for all your needs, the compassionate comforter of all your sadness, the wise guide on your path through life; He is also far more than that, for He will carry you beyond this world into the next.

God saves you with limitless love. He keeps you whole for eternity. He is your future, the source of your eternal being. No one will ever snatch you out of His hand; no one will ever undo what His love has accomplished in your life. That is why the apostle Paul wrote in his first letter to the church at Corinth, "No eye has seen, no ear has heard, and no mind has imagined what God has prepared for those who love him" (1 Corinthians 2:9 NLT). He will make you shine for all eternity!

I am so glad, Lord, that I have all eternity to enjoy Your love.

WITH ALL YOUR HEART, SOUL, AND STRENGTH

Love the Lord your God with all your heart, with all your soul, and with all your strength. These words that I am giving you today are to be in your heart.

DEUTERONOMY 6:5–6 HCSB

God wasn't being too demanding when He placed this claim on your life. Why shouldn't you love your Creator will all your being, since all the good things in your life are God's gifts? Out of nothingness, God's creative grace raised you to the dignity of your true self—that is the foundation of His love-claim on your heart.

You owe all that you are to the Creator who made you, and yet your debt goes even deeper, for He also gave you back yourself when you had lost your true identity. According to the Bible, God simply spoke the world into being (Genesis 1), but to raise you back to your true identity, God entered His creation in the form of Jesus, and He suffered pain and shame. In the first creation, He created your nature and all the world—but in the new creation, He gave you Himself, and by that gift, He restored to you the self you had lost.

What can you possibly give back to God in return for all He has done for you? Yourself!

I give You myself, Lord, for You have given me everything.

ALPHA AND OMEGA

"I am the Alpha and the Omega," says the Lord God,
"who is and who was and who is to come, the Almighty."
REVELATION 1:8 NASB

God stretches throughout all time—and beyond into eternity. Since God has no limits, His love for you has no limits either. This means that you also should set no limits on the love you have for Him. It's not as though your love for God is some little gift you bring out on Sundays or special occasions. Instead, it's the essence of your truest self. It's at the core of who you were created to be.

Since the Supreme Being loves you, the one who has no boundary to His being, neither in time nor in space nor in capacity for love, whose greatness is infinite, whose wisdom is limitless, and whose peace is beyond understanding—since this is the being who loves you, why would you want to hold back anything when you love Him in return?

Alpha and Omega, thank You for loving me for all eternity. May I learn to love You more and more.

UNSELFISH

[Love] is not selfish.
1 CORINTHIANS 13:5 HCSB

If you love something on account of something else, what you really love is that something else. For example, the apostle Paul did not preach the good news as a way to earn his living; instead, he earned his living so that he would have what he needed to preach the good news. What he loved was not his food and lodging but the gospel. True love never demands anything in return. It springs from the soul; it's not a business contract. A contract—"I'll do this if you do that"—never gives birth to love. Love is spontaneous.

So we don't love God for the good that it does us to love Him—and yet God makes sure our love is rewarded. Love itself is the reward! God Himself is our reward.

Lord, thank You that Your love for me is unselfish.
You are totally giving, utterly generous. Teach me to
love You—and others—the way that You love.

THE LORD'S HOUSE

Surely your goodness and love will follow me all the days of my life, and I will dwell in the house of the LORD forever.

PSALM 23:6 NIV

There is nothing that concerns you that doesn't concern God. As you dwell in His house, you are enclosed within His love, a place where His thoughts circle constantly around you, lifting you up like eagle wings (Isaiah 40:31).

Although He loves each human He has created, when you are with Him in your own special dwelling place, it's as though His love is for you alone. He is almighty, so you can trust Him to be able to help you with your problems. And He is all-knowing, so you can have confidence in Him.

All *you* need to do is make the time to be with Him. He is longing to spend time with you. He wants to hear your voice telling Him all that hurts you, all that gives you joy, all that angers you, all that makes you laugh. He wants to hear it all!

Lord, thank You that Your goodness and love are always following me. I want to dwell with You in the special home You've created just for me.

RUNNING IN CIRCLES

Whom have I in heaven but you?
I desire you more than anything on earth.
PSALM 73:25 NLT

Often, instead of relying on God's love, we seek happiness and fulfillment from the created world. We think that if we keep trying new things, eventually we'll find the thing that truly satisfies our hearts. But it never seems to work. No matter how much we have, we always want more. Always discontented, we spend our energy working toward new goals that don't satisfy us once they're achieved. What we already have seems to disappear in the shadow of what we don't have. Ultimately, the world's fleeting pleasures only leave us exhausted—and more anxious and yearning than ever.

Why do we wear ourselves out in such useless effort, wandering in circles, longing for something to meet our needs, when we're neglecting the one thing that could bring us the peace we seek—God's love? We lack nothing when we have God.

Lord, when You see me running in circles, chasing things that will never satisfy me, stop me in my tracks. Bring me back to You. Remind me that Your love alone will give me permanent joy and contentment.

CHEWING AIR

God blesses those who hunger and thirst
for justice, for they will be satisfied.
MATTHEW 5:6 NLT

Taking the path that leads straight to God and His love is the only way your soul will find the natural and essential nourishment it needs. Your soul can't eat money and possessions any more than your mouth can chew air. If you saw a hungry person standing with her mouth open in the wind, inhaling great gulps of air to gratify her empty stomach, you'd think she was crazy. But it's no less silly to think your soul can be satisfied with physical things. The world is full of wonderful physical realities—but they're not meant to satisfy spiritual longings.

"Praise the LORD, my soul. . .who satisfies your desires with good things," wrote the psalmist (Psalm 103:1, 5 NIV). Because of His great love for you, God gives you unlimited bounty in the spiritual realm. He will inspire you to do great things; He'll keep you safe on your path to Him; and He will fill you with strength, joy, and love.

I'm hungering and thirsting for You, Lord God. I don't want to try to chew air anymore. I want to fill myself full with Your love.

ALL THINGS

Likewise the Spirit also helpeth our infirmities: for we know not what we should pray for as we ought: but the Spirit itself maketh intercession for us with groanings which cannot be uttered. And he that searcheth the hearts knoweth what is the mind of the Spirit, because he maketh intercession for the saints according to the will of God. And we know that all things work together for good to them that love God, to them who are the called according to his purpose.

ROMANS 8:26–28 KJV

"Don't worry," people say, "things will work out fine in the end."

That may be true in romantic movies, but we know from experience it's not always the case in real life. People lose jobs; they die from diseases and in car accidents. Pandemics sweep around the world, killing thousands. Addiction destroys lives, and crime tears apart our cities. Not everything works out fine in the end—at least not the end we can see on this side of eternity.

And yet Paul says that he knows everything works together for good! He wasn't expressing meaningless, easy optimism, though. He had experienced his share of suffering, from shipwreck to imprisonment. The circumstances of his life were not "fine" by any definition of that word. But he had confidence that the Spirit was working in all things, teaching us how to pray, teaching us how to live.

---

*Spirit of God, thank You for helping me—
and thank You for working in the world around me.*

CURBING SELFISHNESS

What comes first is the natural body, then the spiritual body comes later.
1 CORINTHIANS 15:46 NLT

The Bible is realistic. You were born with a physical body, and your awareness of yourself and the world around you began there. It's only natural that as a baby you started out life being most concerned with your own body and its needs. But the Bible makes clear that your development shouldn't stop there. If your natural self-interest flows past the banks of healthy survival, it can turn into a flood of addiction to physical pleasures. The way to dam that flood is with love—love for God and for others.

Take care of yourself, by all means, with as much attention as you like—but show that same care and interest to those around you. When you balance your natural selfishness with the needs of others, you keep your selfish urges from becoming destructive, and you keep your life centered on God's love, which will pour into you and through you into the world around you.

God, help me to learn to love others the way You love me. Curb my selfishness with love.

GENEROSITY

If you need wisdom, ask our generous God, and he will give it to you. He will not rebuke you for asking.

JAMES 1:5 NLT

When you share pleasures and belongings with others, rather than keeping them all for yourself, you connect yourself to God's conduit of love. And when you refuse to keep everything for yourself, you have far more to share with those around you. When you practice generous giving, you are demonstrating the sort of love that travels straight and true, without deviations, like an arrow flying toward God, never wavering from its course. This is the way your natural self-love will grow rich enough to embrace the world around you.

But what about when you find yourself in need? Well, should that happen, the Bible instructs you to go directly to God with your needs. Remember, He promised that if you "seek the Kingdom of God above all else," "he will give you everything you need" (Luke 12:31 NLT). Remember, God loves you! He won't fail to take care of you. As you practice caring for others, He will be giving His all to caring for you.

I pray, Lord, that You will give me a more generous spirit. Show me where I can give to others—and I'll trust You to take care of my own needs.

LIVING IN LOVE

God is love. Whoever lives in love lives in God, and God in them.

1 JOHN 4:16 NIV

In the nineteenth century, the German minister Christoph Friedrich Blumhardt wrote:

> *Praise and thanks be to God! God loves the world; now I too want to be filled with love toward all that lives. If Jesus, his Son, is only love, then I want to be only love as well. I am enabled to become a follower of this Son; therefore, together with him, I belong to God; I am loved and I love. And where love is, there is life; and where life is, there is the light of men.*

The way to get to know God better is to love others more. The way to let God's love for you into your life is to love others more. The way to live in God is to live in love.

Lord God, teach me to love as You love. I want to live in You. I want to be filled up with Your love so that You can live in me.

FAITHFUL LOVE

The Lord is faithful, and He will strengthen and protect you from the evil one.

2 THESSALONIANS 3:3 NASB

You learn to love God through His faithfulness to you. When you start out, like all children, you are most concerned with yourself—but as you grow in your relationship with God, you mature. You become a vehicle of His love; your hands do His work on earth.

But we must be careful never to lose track of the fact that we never grow so mature that we're not dependent on God's love, strength, and protection. When things are going smoothly, it's easy to think we're doing it on our own. Perhaps that's one reason troubles and trials come into our lives—so that when our own strength fails us, we turn anew to God for help. We realize all over again how dependent we are on Him.

Because God loves us faithfully, through all life's ups and downs, we can accomplish good things in life—but without Him, we can do nothing.

Thank You, Lord, for Your constant and dependable love. Remind me that without it, I am weak—but with You, I can be strong.

LOVING OTHERS

Now that you have purified yourselves by obeying the truth so that you have sincere love for each other, love one another deeply, from the heart.

1 PETER 1:22 NIV

As you go deeper into a love relationship with God, you'll find yourself also learning to love His entire creation more deeply. This is real love, not just sentiment or fuzzy feel-good feelings. It's love that is based not on words or feelings but on actions.

This is the way we reciprocate God's love—by loving others. When you love others in this way—unselfishly, without thought of being paid back—then you are loving the way God loves you. As with anything else in life, the more you practice this active form of love, the easier and more habitual it becomes. You become free to love without thought of yourself. You can focus on what is best for God's kingdom.

Teach me, Lord, to love more like You love.
I want to show You my love by loving others.

HURT FEELINGS

The LORD is with me; I will not be afraid.
What can mere mortals do to me?
PSALM 118:6 NIV

Life isn't always fair—and people aren't always nice. There will always be someone who is willing to insult you, gossip about you, or belittle your accomplishments. Usually, this sort of meanness stems from jealousy and insecurity, but that doesn't keep it from hurting.

But you have a best friend who is always standing at your side. When others tear you down, remember that their opinions will never matter as much as God's. The Creator of the universe loves you, approves of you, and will defend you. Remember, you are not what others think you are. You are what God created.

When my feelings are hurt, God, remind me that Your love for me never wavers. Be a shield for my wounded heart.

HAND IN HAND WITH GOD

"I hold you by your right hand—I, the Lord your God. And I say to you, 'Don't be afraid. I am here to help you.'"

Isaiah 41:13 NLT

God wants you to know He is with you. He is holding your hand, always walking close beside you, even when you can't sense His presence with you. And as you walk through life hand in hand with God, you can face anything. His love covers you. His presence is your guard.

"Don't be afraid," God says to you. "You're not alone. I'm with you. I will never forget you or abandon you. There is nothing you could do that would erase My love. So stop worrying. Give Me all your fear and anxiety. I want to carry it for you. I want you to know that with My help, you can do all things. I love you so much!"

Sometimes, Lord, I can't feel Your hand in mine. Sometimes I can't hear Your voice. Help me to know—with a soul-deep knowledge—that even when I'm too deaf to hear You, and my vision is too cloudy to see You, You are still there with me. When my hand is too numb to feel Your touch, may I cling to Your promises. When fear strikes my heart, may I cling to Your love.

AGAPE LOVE

The Spirit God gave us does not make us timid,
but gives us power, love and self-discipline.
2 TIMOTHY 1:7 NIV

In *God's Power to Change Your Life*, author Rick Warren writes that "when the Bible speaks of God's love for us and the kind of love we are to have for him and for other people, the word is always *agape*, signifying a commitment to act." That's the word Paul used here in this letter he wrote to his young disciple Timothy—*agape*, a love that has power, that rolls up its sleeves and gets to work.

God's love for you is like that. It's active. It doesn't just wrap you up in warm, rosy feelings; it changes things in your life for the better. And that love working inside you will give you the ability to love others in the same way. You'll make a difference in the world.

Thank You, Lord, that Your love for me is active. It is shaping my life, making it into something new and wonderful. May my love for others also be helpful and useful. I want to make a difference.

PEACE

Do not be anxious about anything, but in every situation, by prayer and petition, with thanksgiving, present your requests to God. And the peace of God, which transcends all understanding, will guard your hearts and your minds in Christ Jesus.

PHILIPPIANS 4:6–7 NIV

God's love is real and present in our lives all the time, no matter what. That means that one of the gifts of His love—peace—is also available to us all the time. His peace is a constant reality, regardless of how much outer conflict we are experiencing at the moment. The world may be full of turmoil, but deep within your heart, God wants you to be at rest, confident of His love.

But just as there are times when clouds hide the sun's constant presence from our eyes, we all have times when life's storms hide God's peace from our senses. In these verses that the apostle Paul wrote to the church at Philippi, he tells us the secret to seeing past the clouds: keep praying. Instead of worrying and dwelling on your troubles, hand them over to God—and He'll give you His peace in return!

Lord, I long for Your peace to stand guard around my heart, protecting me from the fear that besets me. In every situation I encounter, remind me to turn it over to You in prayer.

YOUR ADVOCATE

"When the Father sends the Advocate as my representative—that is, the Holy Spirit—he will teach you everything and will remind you of everything I have told you. I am leaving you with a gift—peace of mind and heart. And the peace I give is a gift the world cannot give. So don't be troubled or afraid."

JOHN 14:26–27 NLT

The Greek word that the New Living Translation uses here—"Advocate"—can also mean "comforter," "helper," "counselor," or "companion." The word refers to someone who enters intimately into a situation, someone with deep insight and wisdom who will be able to give you sound advice and guidance, someone who loves you deeply and will speak up on your behalf.

This aspect of God's nature is pretty amazing if you think about it. The living Spirit of the Creator of the universe is present in your life all the time. There is nothing you need to do to earn that presence. There is no special prayer or magical formula for calling the Holy Spirit—the Spirit is already there, both within you and all around you. Your advocate is not far off, and He doesn't come and go. Instead, He abides with you constantly, bringing with Him the assurance of God's love and the promise of His peace. He will never leave you or forsake you!

Thank You, Holy Spirit, for Your loving presence in my life. I ask that You give me Your peace.

GOOD AS NEW

"People [will exclaim], 'Thank God-of-the-Angel-Armies. He's so good! His love never quits.' . . . I'll restore everything that was lost in this land. I'll make everything as good as new." I, God, say so.

Jeremiah 33:11 MSG

Life wears you down. It breaks you. It robs you of things and people you love. But even when you feel as though you are incomplete, God loves you completely. When you feel broken and imperfect, He loves you perfectly. If you feel lost, God's love will lead you back home. And if you feel worn out, God will make you good as new.

God says so!

God, thank You for Your healing love that restores me to myself. When life is hard, I need more and more of You. I need Your love to mend me and make me new.

A FREE GIFT

By grace are ye saved through faith;
and that not of yourselves: it is the gift of God.
EPHESIANS 2:8 KJV

Sometimes people say (or imply), "Change into a better person—and then God will love you." But that's not the way God's love works. The Bible says that God's love is a free gift, and as you accept His love into your life, you will naturally change into a better person.

The Christian life isn't about working hard to be perfect—and feeling like a failure when you inevitably don't do everything perfectly. No, that's not it at all! As you have an ongoing love relationship with God, you'll experience His love more and more fully so that it makes you whole.

Being a Christian isn't about trying to be someone you're not. It's about letting God's love make you into who you really are.

I am so grateful, Lord, for the free gift of Your love and grace.
Show me how I can make more room for You in my life.

BELIEF VERSUS TRUST

Let not your heart be troubled: ye believe in God, believe also in me.

JOHN 14:1 KJV

Most people believe in God. A 2017 Gallup survey found that as many as 87 percent of all Americans believe in God, and a 2014 survey found that 88 percent of Americans say they believe in God. But believing in God as an abstract concept is not the same as believing in a God who loves you and gives Himself for you.

The word that the King James Version translates as "believe" actually has to do with trust. In today's world, though, it's hard to trust God and not let our hearts be troubled. So many things seem to be going wrong! Trusting when you can't see what God is doing is hard.

But that's what trust is all about. The word *trust* comes from a very ancient root word that meant literally "firm, solid"—and trust requires that you walk out onto God's promises, believing that they are the most solid ground you will ever find upon which to build your life. God longs for you to feel secure in His love. He wants you to have confidence that because He is caring for you, you don't need to be anxious about anything.

God, I don't always understand why You allow events to unfold the way they do. I believe in You—now, help me to trust You.

UNIMAGINABLE

"What no eye has seen, what no ear has heard, and what no human mind has conceived"—the things God has prepared for those who love him.

1 CORINTHIANS 2:9 NIV

This verse refers to the future bounty of blessings that extends into eternity, which God has prepared for us—but it could also refer to the love of God itself. Humans have never seen or heard anything like it; they can't conceive of its limitlessness.

We all tend to reduce God to our own dimensions. Since our love is usually conditional and limited, we think God's must be also. But we need to stop holding on to our ideas *about* God and instead encounter Him for ourselves.

If you multiplied human love by a thousand. . .or a million. . .or a billion, you still wouldn't have a good picture of God's infinite love. His love is a mystery, beyond our expectations, beyond anything we can even imagine.

God of love, I want to stop worshipping my ideas about what You're like; instead, I want to begin to know You as You really are. I know You will always be a mystery to me, but in Your great love and mercy, lead me ever closer to You.

ASK!

"Until now you have not asked for anything in my name.
Ask and you will receive, and your joy will be complete."
JOHN 16:24 NIV

In his book *The Magnificent Defeat*, Frederick Buechner wrote, "If you have never known the power of God's love, then maybe it is because you have never asked to know it—I mean really asked, expecting an answer."

Have you asked God to show you His love? If your life feels gloomy and full of confusion, have you asked God for light? If you feel lonely, worthless, or full of despair, have you asked God to come near?

Try asking. God wants your joy to be complete.

God, I know You promised to answer me when I call—to give me what I need when I ask. So I'm calling. I'm asking. I need You.

LIES

Now this is what the LORD says—the One who created you, Jacob, and the One who formed you, Israel—"Do not fear, for I have redeemed you; I have called you by your name; you are Mine."
ISAIAH 43:1 HCSB

Martin Luther once said, "The sin underneath all our sins is to trust the lie of the serpent that we cannot trust the love and grace of Christ and must take matters into our own hands." In the Garden of Eden, God's love gave Adam and Eve everything they could possibly need—but they fell for the lie the serpent told them. They believed that if they ate the fruit of the tree, they'd be giving themselves something they *really* needed that God hadn't given them.

In our own lives, sometimes it's fear that motivates us. We don't fully trust that we belong to God. We forget that God created us and knows our every need. We act as though we don't belong to Him, and then we decide that we have to go after what we need on our own. Like Adam and Eve, we make the mistake of thinking we need to take matters into our own hands—instead of trusting the one who shaped our very being, who loves us, and who calls us by name.

Forgive me, Lord, when I don't trust You enough. I don't want to believe lies anymore.

FATHER GOD

This resurrection life you received from God is not a timid, grave-tending life. It's adventurously expectant, greeting God with a childlike "What's next, Papa?" God's Spirit touches our spirits and confirms who we really are. We know who he is, and we know who we are: Father and children. And we know we are going to get what's coming to us—an unbelievable inheritance!

ROMANS 8:15–17 MSG

Do you ever look at your life and realize you've been living a timid life, a life that's focused on the graves of old hopes rather than on the challenges and hopes that tomorrow will bring? God doesn't want you to live like that any longer. He wants you to wake up every morning with a child's joy and anticipation, with the delighted assurance that in the twenty-four hours ahead, your Father God has good things planned for you, new blessings to give you.

Some of us have had complicated relationships with our human fathers—but God is the perfect Father, the Father who loves you tenderly, who builds you up and never tears you down, who wants only good for you. Trust His love to do amazing things in your life.

Father God, thank You for Your love that never fails me. Help me to turn away from yesterday's graves and face tomorrow with new hope and joy, knowing that You will always be with me.

RELYING ON GOD

We were crushed and overwhelmed beyond our ability to endure, and we thought we would never live through it. . . . But as a result, we stopped relying on ourselves and learned to rely only on God.

2 CORINTHIANS 1:8–9 NLT

None of us can control all aspects of our lives. We all like to try to figure things out for ourselves. We like to say, "Sure, this is a bad situation, but I think I can see what God is doing through all of this." But then, if we can't see any good that is being accomplished, we start to doubt. *Maybe God doesn't know what He's doing after all*, we think. *Maybe He doesn't really love me.*

That's where faith comes in. When life comes crashing down around you, when you feel overwhelmed, when nothing makes sense, those are the times when you realize how weak you are. You can't rely anymore on your own intelligence and abilities. And those are the moments when you realize how much you need God's love.

God is not punishing you for your lack of faith, and He hates to see you suffer. But He can use this time to build your faith. He helps you to walk forward through all life's challenges, relying totally on the grasp of His hand on yours. He loves you so much that He will bring good out of hardship in ways you never would have thought possible.

Thank You, God, that Your love never stops working in my life.

MARRIED

"I'll marry you for good—forever! I'll marry you true and proper, in love and tenderness. Yes, I'll marry you and neither leave you nor let you go. You'll know me, God, for who I really am."

Hosea 2:19–20 MSG

Human marriage is a beautiful picture of God's love—but sadly, we all know of some marriages that didn't last. Human marriages can fall apart, ending up in broken hearts, separation, and divorce.

But that will never happen with God. When He "marries" you, it's for good, for always. He'll never leave you—and if you leave Him, He'll keep pursuing you, wooing you until you're back home, once more sharing His love.

God, thank You for loving me so faithfully. Even when I am unfaithful to You, You never give up on me. Help me get to know You better and better.

CONFIDENCE

When I am afraid, I will put my trust in You.
In God, whose word I praise, in God I have put my trust;
I shall not be afraid. What can mere mortals do to me?
PSALM 56:3–4 NASB

Sometimes we forget that the people who wrote the Bible were living, breathing human beings much like ourselves. Three thousand years ago, David wrote this psalm when the Philistines had seized him in Gath. These Philistines had been enemies of the Israelites for a long time, and they no doubt remembered that when David was still a teenager, he had killed their giant, Goliath. David had good reason to be afraid—and yet he was able to sing these words to God.

David hadn't forgotten Goliath either. His past experience with God gave him confidence in the present moment of danger. With only five stones and a slingshot, he had brought down a giant—but only because he had called on God to help him. Now, in this new crisis, he had faith that God would once more come through for him.

If you are new in your love relationship, it may be easy to doubt that God's love will come through for you. But the longer you stick with God, the more experience you'll gain in His love. With each new crisis, you'll grow more confident that you can put your trust in Him.

Dear Lord, when I am afraid, remind me to be like David and put my trust in You. What can mere humans do to me when I'm wrapped in Your love?

PLANTED IN LOVE

With both feet planted firmly on love, you'll be able to take in with all followers of Jesus the extravagant dimensions of Christ's love. Reach out and experience the breadth! Test its length! Plumb the depths! Rise to the heights! Live full lives, full in the fullness of God. God can do anything, you know—far more than you could ever imagine or guess or request in your wildest dreams! He does it not by pushing us around but by working within us, his Spirit deeply and gently within us.

EPHESIANS 3:17–20 MSG

What do you think it means to plant your feet firmly on love? It sounds as though there's an element of choice going on, a firm commitment on your part, a complete and utter dedication to make love the foundation of your life. When you do that, this verse promises, your life will change. You'll begin to experience just how generous God's love truly is. His love will fill your life to overflowing. And this change will happen from the inside out as God's Spirit works within you.

I want to live life to its fullest, Lord. Help me to plant my feet firmly on love so that I can experience all that You have planned for me, the full abundance of Your great love, Your extravagant blessings.

GOD'S WILL

"May your will be done on earth, as it is in heaven."
MATTHEW 6:10 NLT

If you can empty yourself even for an instant, allowing yourself to be lost in God, then you have experienced a moment of heaven. Most of us can only hold on to a mere moment of such joy—and then everyday life comes rushing back. Just as we feel we might float away in the utter bliss of God's love, we get dragged back to earth.

That's only natural—it happens to even the greatest "saints"—but this is when your willpower comes into play. No matter how you're feeling emotionally, you can choose to seek God's way instead of your own. As you do, you'll find true happiness, because gratifying your own selfish impulses never makes you happy for very long. Your greatest joy will come from praying each day, "Your will be done, Lord." This way of living puts you in the place where you'll be free to experience God's love most fully.

God, I choose Your way, not mine.

LOVE GIFTS

Every good thing given and every perfect gift is from above, coming down from the Father of lights, with whom there is no variation or shifting shadow.

JAMES 1:17 NASB

All the things in life that comfort you, delight you, and give you pleasure are gifts from God. You are surrounded by His gifts. The food you eat, the water you drink, the very air you breathe, all are love gifts from His generous and creative Spirit. God has wrapped you in His love. He encloses you with tenderness. Everywhere you turn, His love is there. And He will never change His mind. He'll never abandon you.

I am grateful, Lord God, that Your love never changes or shifts. Thank You for the countless gifts of love You have given to me.

THE TRANSLATION OF GOD'S LOVE

"I am the resurrection and the life. The one who believes in me will live, even though they die; and whoever lives by believing in me will never die. Do you believe this?"

John 11:25–26 NIV

Again and again in the Gospels, Jesus says, "I am. . . ." When He does this, He's affirming that His own personality and character complete the "I Am" God gave Moses so many centuries earlier when Moses asked God for His name (Exodus 3:13–14). Jesus translates the name of God into a language we can more easily understand. He reveals to us the invisible, all-loving Creator of the universe. If any ideas we have about God are contrary to what we see in Jesus, then we need to let go of those thoughts and ask Jesus to replace them with the truth of His being.

Jesus shows you a God who satisfies your hunger, sheds light into your darkness, opens up new opportunities, lays down His own life for you, and gives you endless, abundant love. Nowhere in all the Gospels does Jesus ever say, "I am a stern and cruel taskmaster"! Nor does He say, "I am far away from people, and I don't care about their suffering." Instead, Jesus shows you again and again a God who loves you.

When I'm filled with doubt and fear, Lord Jesus, show me Your face. Remind me that You are the translation of God's love for me.

OLD AGE

"I'll keep on carrying you when you're old.
I'll be there, bearing you when you're old and gray."
ISAIAH 46:4 MSG

You've probably heard the saying "Old age is not for sissies." Although modern medicine and a healthy diet can help many of us live active, productive lives for longer than our ancestors could, eventually our bodies will begin to wear out. Aches and pains may begin to plague us; we won't have the strength and stamina we once had.

Our identities are so tied up with our bodies that it's difficult to let go of their abilities and appearance. But God will have love gifts to give us even at this last stage of our lives. He will bless us in new ways. He'll carry us in His arms all the way to eternity.

Oh God, thank You that You will be with me in my old age. Help me not to fear this last stage of my life. I trust that You will be with me, bearing me up through whatever happens.

GRACE THAT'S SUFFICIENT

My grace is sufficient for thee: for my strength is made perfect in weakness.
2 CORINTHIANS 12:9 KJV

Throughout the Bible, grace is something that connects God's heart and ours. It is powerful; it changes both our inner and outer lives. It is the Spirit of God present in our lives. And if you have eyes to see, you'll find God's grace everywhere you turn. Grace shines in the sunlight; it touches your life through a neighbor's smile or a child's laughter; it warms your heart in acts of unexpected kindness from a passing stranger. And you'll also find it inside your own heart. It is the capacity to be kind when you thought you'd used up all your patience; it is the strength you find inside yourself to make a change for the good; it is your ability to love someone who has hurt you.

Always, God's grace is something that is freely given. There is nothing you can do to earn it. It just shows up in your life, undeserved. It is the expression of divine love, flowing constantly into your life. It will give you everything you need, even when you feel as though you're at your weakest.

I'm glad, God, that I don't have to be strong or good or beautiful or anything else to receive Your grace. When I feel as though there are so many things I want that I don't have, remind me that Your grace is always enough.

YOUR BODY

God causes everything to work together
for the good of those who love God.
ROMANS 8:28 NLT

Our bodies may sometimes seem to be the cause of all our stumbling, but in reality, our bodies and our spirits depend on each other. Both are gifts of love from God. Even though our bodies are fragile, temporary organisms, they give living essence to our spirits during our time on earth. They work together with our spirits, part of God's great plan for wholeness.

The body doesn't have to be a stumbling block; it can be a stepping stone toward God. Even when your body seems like a burden, it is actually helping your spirit grow. God gave your body to you because He loves you. It works together with your spirit for good.

Thank You for my body, Lord, and for the ways in which it works together with my spirit. May I use it as a stepping stone toward You.

THE LAW OF THE LORD

"Love your neighbor as yourself; I am the Lord."
Leviticus 19:18 NASB

When we are preoccupied by our own self-interest, we are isolating ourselves, both from others and from God. It's like choosing to live in a dark, dusty corner of a room, when we could be enjoying the wide-open light and fellowship that God offers us.

This is the Lord's law: that each of us seek not our own good but one another's. It is called the "law of the Lord" not only because it is what God wants for us, but also because we can never achieve it without God's help—and because it is the description of God's own nature. Love by definition gives itself away. And God is love.

Love is the eternal law that created the universe and continues to rule it. Nothing exists outside love.

Help me, Lord, to always follow Your law of love.

YOUR GOD

"Be strong. Take courage. Don't be intimidated. Don't give [your enemies] a second thought because God, your God, is striding ahead of you. He's right there with you. He won't let you down; he won't leave you."

Deuteronomy 31:6 MSG

Notice that this verse refers to God as "your God." There's something very intimate about that. He's not a generic god who gives generic blessings. No, He is *your* God, and He gives you blessings intended just for you.

So be strong. Take courage. Don't be intimidated by whoever or whatever your enemies are. An enemy could be a coworker who talks about you behind your back, or it could be depression, or a lack of self-confidence, or a painful physical condition that won't go away. Whatever your enemy is, God is right there with you, facing it. Even more, He goes ahead of you, preparing the way for you, so that what you fear so much is already taken care of by His loving hand. The Creator of the universe dwells in you and outside of you, constantly available to encourage you and help you. He won't let you down.

Thank You, Lord of love, that I don't need to worry about anything anymore. Instead, I can give everything to You, trusting Your love to take care of each detail of my life. Thank You that You are my God.

MISSING THE TARGET

There is no condemnation for those who belong to Christ Jesus.
ROMANS 8:1 NLT

In the New Testament, the literal meaning of the Greek word that our Bibles translate as "sin" is "to miss the target." The image is of an arrow that fails to hit the bull's-eye—and instead flies off into the grass.

We all have times we totally miss the target. Sometimes we did the best we could and we still failed. Other times we chose not to even aim at the target. Either way, afterward we feel ashamed and sorry.

But God's love doesn't leave us drowning in shame. Because of Jesus, we don't have to feel guilty and condemned. We're free to try again and do better next time.

Thank You, Jesus, for taking away my shame. When I'm tempted to wallow in it, remind me to turn to You. Take my guilt away—and help me to do better.

STRENGTH TO FLY

Those who trust in the Lord will find new strength. They will soar high on wings like eagles. They will run and not grow weary. They will walk and not faint.

Isaiah 40:31 NLT

There are so many demands on your strength. So many crises to confront, so many problems to solve, so many people who need your help. No wonder you feel exhausted sometimes. No wonder there are days when you'd like to just give up, when you've reached the end of your strength.

And yet when you acknowledge your own weakness, that's the exact moment the Holy Spirit can begin to work in your life in new ways. The Bible is full of assurances you can turn to when you feel too weak to go on. It promises that you can do all things through Christ who gives you strength (Philippians 4:13), that your strength comes from God's might (Ephesians 6:10), that the Spirit will help you when you are weak (Romans 8:26), and that God's grace will always be enough, giving you the strength you need to keep going even when it seems impossible (2 Corinthians 12:9).

When you throw up your own hands, God's hands have room to work. He can help you not just survive but thrive. You won't find merely the strength to keep staggering along; you'll be able to run. You'll be able to fly! That's how much He loves you.

When I am too weak to keep going, remind me, Lord, that Your love will carry me.

THE VINE

"Live in me. Make your home in me just as I do in you. In the same way that a branch can't bear grapes by itself but only by being joined to the vine, you can't bear fruit unless you are joined with me."
JOHN 15:4 MSG

Notice that this verse says that Jesus is making His home in you. Now it's up to you to make your home in Him. When you do, you make room for His love to fill you up. He is the vine, and you are a branch that gets its life from Him. His love is like the sap that flows into you, bringing you to life. Because of Him, your life will bear fruit. His love will flow through you and out into the world.

Live in Jesus. And you'll change the world.

Jesus, thank You for Your love flowing into me with life and strength and health. Help me to bear fruit for You.

HE'S ALWAYS LISTENING

They called on the name of Baal from morning till noon. "Baal, answer us!" they shouted. But there was no response; no one answered. And they danced around the altar they had made. At noon Elijah began to taunt them. "Shout louder!" he said. "Surely he is a god! Perhaps he is deep in thought, or busy, or traveling. Maybe he is sleeping and must be awakened." So they shouted louder and slashed themselves with swords and spears, as was their custom, until their blood flowed. Midday passed, and they continued their frantic prophesying until the time for the evening sacrifice. But there was no response, no one answered, no one paid attention.

1 KINGS 18:26–29 NIV

Trusting God means trusting His love for you—rather than trusting in your love for God. You don't have to be like the prophets of Baal, whipping up your emotions into a frenzy in order to get God to hear you.

When you come to God in prayer, don't worry if sometimes (or even many times) you don't feel much emotionally. He doesn't need you to convince Him that you love Him. Instead, He wants to convince you of how much He loves you.

Lord, thank You that You are always listening to me, always loving me, no matter how I feel.

ARMOR

Be strong in the Lord and in his mighty power.
Put on the full armor of God.
EPHESIANS 6:10–11 NIV

Do you ever feel fragile? Maybe some days you sail through life confidently—but then there are the days when everything seems to go wrong. People hurt your feelings, even when they don't mean to. You make stupid mistakes, and you feel embarrassed and ashamed. The world keeps bumping into you, and every time, you go flying.

When you feel like that, it's time to put on your armor—the love of God. Wrap yourself in it. Make sure it covers every inch of you. And then go out into the world clothed in God's strength and power.

When I feel fragile, Lord, remind me that Your armor is always available for me to wear. Clothe me in Your love.

BASKING IN GOD'S LOVE

"You are altogether beautiful, my darling, and there is no blemish on you."
SONG OF SOLOMON 4:7 NASB

When we look into our mirrors, we're likely to focus on every bump, lump, and wrinkle. We see every pimple, every frizz, every bulge.

But that's not how God sees you. When He looks at you, He sees someone who is completely, totally beautiful. He doesn't see a single blemish!

It's so hard to believe, God, that You can look at me and see a completely beautiful person. I'm so aware of all my faults. When I watch television or leaf through a magazine, I feel like my body just doesn't measure up. And inside, I'm not much better. I'm selfish, I'm too sensitive, I get preoccupied with the wrong things. Help me to set all that aside. Today I want to simply bask in Your love.

DOUBT

There has never been the slightest doubt in my mind that the God who started this great work in you would keep at it and bring it to a flourishing finish on the very day Christ Jesus appears.
PHILIPPIANS 1:6 MSG

If you don't trust God, you won't be able to believe in His love. You may say you believe God is love—but your emotions will tell you something else. Deep inside, you may believe God is frightening or far away. You doubt He'll do anything to help you. You fear that He might even do something to hurt you.

Trust is essential to any relationship, whether with God or with another human being. Most of us learned to trust as babies; we cried, and our parents came to our aid, teaching us that we could count on them to be there when we needed them. But sometimes parents fail to teach their children how to trust. If our parents hurt us, we may not be able to trust others, including God. Or maybe a close friend or a spouse damaged our trust later in life. When someone who is important to us lets us down, we learn to distrust others. We find it hard to trust even God. We are constantly on guard, trying to protect ourselves against hurt.

If that's true for you, don't worry that God will get mad at you. He understands your doubts. His love is patient. And the more you experience His love, the fewer doubts you'll have.

Lord, I give You all my doubts. Thank You for being so patient with me.

A WORLD OF LOVE

"Love your enemies, do good to those who hate you."
LUKE 6:27 NASB

If you cut yourself off from the person who offends you, who doesn't understand you, who regularly humiliates or scolds you, are you participating in God's love? It's one thing to set up healthy boundaries; God doesn't expect you to be anyone's doormat. But be aware of what your ultimate goal is.

As Christ's followers, we are each called to work for a world of love—a place where the consequences of hatred and prejudice are healed, where we work together to build a world of justice for all people. This is long, hard work, requiring great patience, determination, and courage. But when we commit ourselves to this work, we are working hand in hand with the Spirit of love. We are allowing God's love, which He so freely gives, to flow through us.

Give me strength, Lord, to work with Your Spirit. Help me to set aside my sense of personal injury and annoyance. Help me to look past the differences that seem so important; let me see with Your eyes. Show me what I can do to build a better world.

PRACTICE MAKES PERFECT

Trust God from the bottom of your heart; don't try to figure out everything on your own. Listen for God's voice in everything you do, everywhere you go; he's the one who will keep you on track.

PROVERBS 3:5–6 MSG

Placing your trust in someone you can't see or touch can sometimes feel like walking blind. For all you know a giant precipice is yawning up ahead; when you take a step, you may go tumbling down into nothingness. Trust and love are bound up together—but it's hard to trust someone you don't really know.

Like almost everything in life, though, trust takes practice—and the more you practice, the easier it becomes. As you stop relying so much on your own selfish wants and wishes, and instead begin turning to God for guidance, you'll find that your life goes differently. As you grow in your love for God, His love for you will blossom in your heart. That love will give you confidence; trust will come more easily to you. And each time you trust God, you'll see what His love accomplishes in your life. Next time, it will be a little easier to rely on God's guidance. Eventually, trust becomes a habit. God's love will be the path you follow.

God, I want to grow closer and closer to You. I want to get to know You better and better. I know when that happens, I'll be able to trust You more completely.

SPENDING TIME WITH GOD

Don't worry about anything; instead, pray about everything. Tell God what you need, and thank him for all he has done.

PHILIPPIANS 4:6 NLT

Imagine a beloved friend you talk to daily. You don't spend hours with her every day, but you set aside as much time as you can to spend together. Throughout the day, even while you're both busy with other things, you often send each other a quick text message or email. If a crisis were to occur, you'd let her know immediately because you'd want her support and understanding—and you know she would drop everything to listen.

Now imagine you shut down that open channel of communication between you and your friend. Days go by without the two of you communicating, and then weeks and even months. Before long, you probably wouldn't feel close to her. You might still care about her, but changes in both your lives would now come between you. As you stopped sharing the important things in your lives, you began to grow apart. The love between the two of you has cooled.

The same is true of your relationship with God. The only way to be close to Him is to spend time with Him and talk with Him often. The more you do that, the more confident you will be of His love—and the less you'll worry.

I love You, Lord. Let's spend more time together today.

AT HOME

"Make yourselves at home in my love. If you keep my commands, you'll remain intimately at home in my love."
JOHN 15:9–10 MSG

Lovers who are confident of each other's faithfulness and love feel at home in each other's presence. In fact, wherever that beloved other person is may feel like home, whether it's a house you share, a hotel room on a vacation, or a strange place on the other side of the world—so long as you're together, you're home.

Jesus wants you to feel that same sense of "at-homeness" with Him. And He has given you the key to feeling that way—keeping His commands. These aren't a complicated list of rules, a long catalog of do's and don'ts. No, His only commands are to love God with all your heart, mind, and soul, and to love others the way you love yourself.

It's that simple—and that hard. But as you learn to live this way, loving both God and others with everything you have to give, you'll find yourself feeling more and more at home in Jesus' love. You'll have a steady love relationship with God.

Jesus, help me to love others the way You do—and help me as well to love the Father the way You do. I want to walk in Your footsteps. I want to be at home in Your love.

THE BODY OF JESUS

Just as the body is one and yet has many parts, and all the parts of the body, though they are many, are one body, so also is Christ. For by one Spirit we were all baptized into one body.

1 CORINTHIANS 12:12–13 NASB

Once, Jesus walked the earth in a body like ours. But now through the Holy Spirit, *we* are the body of Jesus. You are a part of that body. You carry Jesus out into the world.

That means you are called to be a visible manifestation of God's love. Because God calls you beloved, you have love to give to others in a variety of ways, big and small. When people tell you their troubles, for example, you can listen carefully, with compassion and genuine interest. You don't need to have the answers. When you see someone who looks sad, even a stranger, you can give them a smile and a kind word. When you see something that's not right, you can speak up.

Through you, others can see Jesus.

Help me, Jesus, to carry Your love to each person I encounter today.

DEPRESSION

The Lord is near to the brokenhearted and saves those who are crushed in spirit.
Psalm 34:18 NASB

According to psychologists, depression that lasts for days is far more than a sad feeling. It's an illness, as real as the flu, that causes a persistent feeling of sadness. Researchers have found that depression is the most common of all psychiatric disorders. Almost all of us, at one time or another in our lives, will experience it. When we do, we can't just "snap out of it."

When we're depressed, we lose interest in life. Depression affects how we feel, think, and behave, and it can lead to a variety of other emotional and physical problems. We may have trouble doing our normal day-to-day activities; we may even feel as if life isn't worth living. Depression can take a toll on our social lives, our professional lives, our spiritual lives, and our physical health. Depression can cast a cloud over our hearts and minds. From within that cloud, it's hard to believe God loves us.

As Christians we may feel we should be immune to depression. But depression is no sin! God has promised us He will be especially close to us when we go through these bleak times. He will be there at our side, His love suffering alongside us as He waits to lead us into His joy once more.

Oh Lord, thank You that Your love surrounds me always, even when I'm deep in depression.

GREAT THINGS

Fear not, O land; be glad and rejoice: for the LORD will do great things.
JOEL 2:21 KJV

Because God loves us so much, He longs to do great things in our lives. But sometimes we get in His way.

Think about a coffee cup sitting on the kitchen counter, clean and empty, just waiting for you to pour your morning brew. That's how we need to come to God—open and ready to receive what He wants to pour into our lives. Now though, imagine someone has placed a plate over that cup. When you stumble into the kitchen with sleep-fogged eyes and pour out the coffeepot, the coffee will come out just fine—there's no problem with your coffeemaker—but instead of filling the cup, the hot liquid will flow onto the counter and floor. Or what if the coffee cup were already filled with stones when you tried to pour your coffee? Some of the coffee would still trickle down into the cup, but there wouldn't be any room for the full measure you were hoping to drink.

When we refuse to surrender our lives to God, they're like those coffee cups. His love is as real and present as ever. He's pouring out blessing upon blessing. . .but we keep getting in His way.

God, I want my life to overflow with Your abundant love and blessing. Point out anything in me that's getting in the way of the great things You want to do in me.

DO THE WORK

"Be strong and courageous, and do the work.
Don't be afraid or discouraged, for the Lord *God,*
my God, is with you. He will not fail you or forsake you."
1 Chronicles 28:20 NLT

We all have times when we feel discouraged. We don't feel strong, and we're overcome with anxiety. We don't *feel* God's loving presence with us.

But this verse tells us that those are the very times we should get busy. We can *act* as though we're strong and courageous, even if that's not the way we feel. We can do the work, regardless of our emotions.

And when we step out in faith, even if it's the smallest of baby steps, God comes to meet us. He will not fail or forsake us.

Lord God, help me to do Your work, no matter what my emotions tell me. Thank You that You are always waiting to help. Thank You that Your love will never fail me.

DISCIPLINE

My dear child, don't shrug off God's discipline, but don't be crushed by it either. It's the child he loves that he disciplines; the child he embraces, he also corrects. God is educating you; that's why you must never drop out. He's treating you as dear children. This trouble you're in isn't punishment; it's training, the normal experience of children.

HEBREWS 12:5–8 MSG

When bad things come into our lives—from little frustrations to major tragedies—they are never God's punishments. That's not the way God acts. His love never punishes.

Instead, sometimes these things are the consequences of our own actions. Other times, they're simply the result of living in a fallen world, where bad things do happen. God's love always surrounds us, but He doesn't allow us to sail through life without dealing with the world's realities.

But when these things happen, God always has something to teach us through the experience. That's what "discipline" really is; it's the teaching that a disciple receives from her master. It's the instruction that helps the disciple become more and more like the teacher.

Lord, I want to be more like You—so when hard times enter my life, remind me to learn whatever You want to teach me from them.

DISCRIMINATION

Whoever claims to love God yet hates a brother or sister is a liar. For whoever does not love their brother and sister, whom they have seen, cannot love God, whom they have not seen.

1 JOHN 4:20 NIV

The literal meaning of the Greek word that is translated "hate" in this verse is "discriminate." In other words, you may not think you hate anyone—but if you think someone is less worthy of your love, if you judge a person or group of people as being problematic in some way, then you are separating yourself from God, who loves all equally.

This is a challenging idea. Today's world is so polarized, with so many groups of "us" set against groups of "them," that it's hard not to fall into the discrimination that the Bible condemns. But John makes himself clear: if you can't love others, whom you can see, don't expect to be able to love God whom you can't see.

Help me, Lord, not to discriminate. Make me sensitive to this tendency in me. I don't want anything to separate me from Your love.

THE PALMS OF GOD'S HANDS

"See, I have written your name on the palms of my hands."
ISAIAH 49:16 NLT

When you were a teenager, did you ever write the name of the person you "liked" on your hand? It's a very adolescent thing to do—and yet this is what God says He's done: He's written your name on the palms of His hands. He loves you that much.

In this verse, God is saying that your name—your very identity—is inscribed on His very being. Your name is written on God.

Imagine that!

Lord, now that I know I'm written on the palms of Your hands, I want to write Your name on me. Not literally, but figuratively, so that I cover every inch of my skin with the name of God. Inscribe Yourself on my heart, on my flesh. Be a part of my very being.

THE LOST SHEEP

"When he has found it, he puts it on his shoulders, rejoicing. And when he comes home, he calls together his friends and his neighbors, saying to them, 'Rejoice with me, because I have found my sheep that was lost!'"

LUKE 15:5–6 NASB

Jesus, who told us this story about a lost sheep, makes it clear that God cares about the individual. His love is not generic; it's personal, particular, intimate. He doesn't love humanity as one great indistinguishable group. He yearns after each of us in particular, and He longs for our presence. He loves the individual.

He loves *you*.

Jesus, thank You that when I am lost, Your love never stops searching for me. Thank You that You love me as an individual, that I am special to You.

A MOTHER'S COMFORT

"As a mother comforts her child, so will I comfort you."
ISAIAH 66:13 NIV

When a child is sick or in trouble, something within the mother changes. She sets aside her busy life, and all her focus, all her energy, shifts to her child as she yearns to help and to heal.

In this verse, God is saying that He loves you the way a mother loves her child. When He sees you suffering in any way, the very nature of His Being is to rush to you. He yearns to help and to heal.

But God is not a human mother with limitations. His patience is unending, His love is unfailing, His healing is powerful, and His comfort is absolute.

Dear God, I'm so grateful for Your tender care. When I am in pain, whether it's physical or emotional, remind me that You are always right there, Your arms held out, longing to pick me up and comfort me.

UNDESERVED LOVE

You received God's Spirit when he adopted you as his own children. Now we call him, "Abba, Father."
ROMANS 8:15 NLT

Children don't earn their parents' love, and parents don't love their children because they deserve to be loved. They don't love their children because they try to be good. They don't love them "in spite of themselves." They simply love them because they are their children.

God loves you in the same way. You have done nothing, nor do you need to do anything, to make Him love you. You don't have to try to be good to earn His love. He understands that like the apostle Paul, you often have to say, "The good that I would I do not: but the evil which I would not, that I do" (Romans 7:19 KJV). Like all good parents, He wants to guide you into healthy, life-giving paths. He sorrows when you go astray and cause yourself needless suffering. But He loves you simply because you are His child.

I am so glad, Abba Father, that I am Your child. I want to live in a way that pleases You—but You know how often I fail. Thank You that there is nothing I need to do to earn Your love.

FREE LOVE

"Freely you have received."
MATTHEW 10:8 NIV

God's love for you will never coerce you into responding. He gives it to you so freely that He creates freedom within you. When you return God's love, you do so not because it's your duty or obligation but out of freedom.

And it is always your choice. You can choose to resist God's love. You can deny Him; you can crucify Him, as human beings have done over and over down through the centuries. This is the terrible risk God takes. He makes Himself completely vulnerable. His love refuses to overpower you. He loves you so much that He gives you your freedom.

Thank You, Lord of love, for the freedom You have given me. Help me to love You more and more—not out of a sense of duty, because I "should" love You, but freely.

GRACE WINS

God's grace and order wins.
Psalm 10:16 MSG

Do you ever look around at the world and wonder where God is? From pandemics to human violence, from polarized politics to natural catastrophes, sometimes it's hard to see the presence of God in our world.

But over and over the Bible deals with situations like this, times of crisis when God's people must have thought everything was falling apart. And over and over the Bible assures us that God is in control. For a time we may see only chaos and destruction—but eventually, God's grace always wins. Nothing can defeat His love.

Lord, help me to be a vehicle of Your grace and love today. In a world that seems to be falling apart, show me how to do my part to spread Your order.

TRIBULATION

"These things I have spoken to you so that in Me you may have peace. In the world you have tribulation, but take courage; I have overcome the world."

John 16:33 NASB

Why do we struggle with the fact that God loves us unconditionally? Why do we feel as though when painful things come into our lives, His love must have wavered?

Because we're thinking of human love. All of us have experienced the pain of someone we love letting us down. If we have had too many of those experiences, or if they became ingrained in us when we were very young, we are all the more likely to attribute to God human tendencies. We assume that He loves the way people do.

But that's not how God's love works. When tribulation comes, it's not a sign that God doesn't love you. Instead, that's the very moment when He is longing to give you more and more of His love so that you can rest in Him. He wants you to know His peace.

Help me, Lord, to understand Your love better. I want to rest in Your peace.

HUMBLE LOVE

But ask the animals, and they will instruct you; ask the birds of the sky, and they will tell you. Or speak to the earth, and it will instruct you; let the fish of the sea inform you.

JOB 12:7–8 HCSB

God is not too proud to use any means possible to speak to you of His love. He doesn't wait for you to hear about His love from some eloquent and intelligent speaker; He doesn't bide His time waiting for you to read the book that will make His love clear to you. Instead, He spills out His love everywhere—in a falling leaf, in the scent of a flower, in the scarlet flash of a cardinal at a bird feeder, or in the wag of a dog's tail.

His love is so patient and humble that nothing is too small for Him to use to convey His message to you—and eternity is not too long for it to take!

Oh God, thank You, thank You, thank You for Your humble, patient love that is everywhere I turn, in everything I see and touch and taste and hear.

BURIED TREASURE

Cast your burden upon the Lord and He will sustain you.

Psalm 55:22 NASB

When Jesus was on the earth, He did not pull back from troubles; instead, He fully experienced even the wickedness of this world, including enemies, violence, and death. He could do so because He knew He would find His Father's love in every situation He faced. He strode fearlessly into the worst the world could offer, knowing He had a loving Father who would carry His burdens and sustain Him.

Can you do the same? Can you cast all your troubles onto the Lord—and seek God in whatever situation you are in? It's a little like finding buried treasure in the midst of a field of mud. Even in the worst circumstances, you can discover the love of the Lord.

Okay, God, I'll give You all my burdens to carry as I face the crises of my life. I'll rely on You to sustain me—and I'll look for Your love hidden even here.

STEADFAST IN HIS LOVE

Surely the righteous will never be shaken. . . . They will have no fear of bad news; their hearts are steadfast, trusting in the Lord.

Psalm 112:6–7 NIV

The only thing that stays the same is that nothing stays the same. Cars break down and need to be repaired—often when we can least afford it. Our bodies grow older, and eventually, they too break down. People we love become ill; sometimes they die. Doors we had hoped to enter slam shut instead. Changes like these are painful. When we hear of yet another change coming, it feels like bad news. We cry out to God and ask, "Why?"

Disruptive changes come to all our lives, but God can use even the most painful of them as an opportunity to show us His love. In the midst of each change, His love never wavers. He is the only unshakable rock on which we can build our lives.

Life is shaky. Just when we think everything is stable, things start to shift and move. But God doesn't waver. His loves stands firm.

God, when everywhere I turn I see change coming, when my world is filled with bad news, remind me that You never change. Thank You that even in the midst of the most painful changes, You are working. Make me steadfast in Your love.

THE ARMOR OF LOVE

Therefore put on the full armor of God, so that when the day of evil comes, you may be able to stand your ground, and after you have done everything, to stand. Stand firm then, with the belt of truth buckled around your waist, with the breastplate of righteousness in place, and with your feet fitted with the readiness that comes from the gospel of peace. In addition to all this, take up the shield of faith, with which you can extinguish all the flaming arrows of the evil one. Take the helmet of salvation and the sword of the Spirit, which is the word of God.

EPHESIANS 6:13–17 NIV

The apostle Paul wrote these words to the church at Ephesus to encourage them to stand firm in the midst of troubling times. He describes in detail the armor that a loving God gives to us to empower us to face even the most confusing and painful circumstances.

The nineteenth-century missionary Christoph Friedrich Blumhardt once wrote, "God's love strides unswerving through everything, like a hero, and will not be insulted, despised, or rejected; it marches through the world with the helmet of hope on its head." Nothing can stop God's love—and nothing can stop you when you're wearing His armor.

Today I want to wear the armor of Your love, Lord.

THE VICTOR

Wake up, O Lord! Why do you sleep? Get up! Do not reject us forever. Why do you look the other way? Why do you ignore our suffering and oppression? . . . Rise up! Help us!

PSALM 44:23–24, 26 NLT

We all have moments when we feel as though God might be sleeping, or at least that His attention is focused on something else. Why else would such terrible things happen, both in our personal lives and in the world at large?

God's love, though, asks us to believe that Jesus' ultimate act of love, His death on the cross, won the victory not over sin as a generic thing, but over individual acts of violence, of arrogance, of prejudice, and of hatred. God is not ignoring these things. Despite appearances, faith in Jesus insists that all these things have been defeated. The power of God's love is stronger than they are.

Strengthen my faith, Jesus, in Your work on the cross. When everywhere I turn I see suffering and oppression, remind me that You are the victor who is conquering all these things.

WALLS

I cry out to the Lord; I plead for the Lord's mercy. I pour out my complaints before him and tell him all my troubles. . . . Then I pray to you, O Lord. I say, "You are my place of refuge. You are all I really want in life. Hear my cry, for I am very low. . . . Bring me out of prison so I can thank you."

Psalm 142:1–2, 5–7 NLT

When the psalmist David wrote these words, he had taken refuge from his enemies in a cave—but now he realized that his safe place had turned into a prison. Lonely, scared, and overwhelmed, he called out to God, confident that God's love would never abandon him.

Sometimes we, like David, find that what we thought was a place of safety has turned into a prison cell. When we can't feel God's love, it could be because we've built walls to protect our vulnerable hearts. But walls not only keep things safe inside; they can also trap you in a place where you no longer sense God's love.

David knew now that his own attempts to find safety had been a waste of time and effort. All he really needed as his refuge was the love of his Lord.

When I wonder where Your love has gone, dear Lord, remind me to check to see if I've been building walls around my heart.

STRONG HEARTS

My health may fail, and my spirit may grow weak,
but God remains the strength of my heart; he is mine forever.
PSALM 73:26 NLT

Sometimes we fill our minds with all that is wrong in our lives. We focus on health problems; we ponder our worries about the world; we pick at the sores of our emotional wounds; we may even mull over our own sinfulness. When we do that, our spirits grow weak, and yet for some reason we hold on so tightly to that which robs us of our strength.

Nothing ever comes of staring at your sins and sorrows. Instead, look at God. Focus on His love for you. When you do that, He will become the strength of your heart.

Lord, when my thoughts begin to dwell on the negatives of my life, turn my attention back to You. I am depending on You to make me strong.

BELIEF AND UNBELIEF

Lord, I believe; help thou mine unbelief.
MARK 9:24 KJV

As much as you want to believe that God loves you, sometimes that reality is just so hard to comprehend. A good technique to combat unbelief is to begin each day, as soon as you wake up, by saying to yourself: *God loves me.* These three little words hold immense strength. Repeat them to yourself throughout your day, whenever you have a little pause in your life (at a traffic light, waiting in line at a store, in the shower, as you fall asleep—wherever and whenever you can).

As you repeat this short sentence, the thought will expand in your consciousness, giving you new energy, joy, and hope. Do it long enough, and it will become habitual, a source of ongoing strength and reassurance that will help you face each challenging situation that comes along.

You love me, Lord. Give me a nudge, I pray, when I forget that amazing fact. May it become the foundation of my life.

THE REALM OF LOVE

Judge not according to the appearance.
JOHN 7:24 KJV

Do you want to dwell in God's love as a citizen of His kingdom? Then you need to stop judging others, because that sets you outside His kingdom of love. You may think you're not guilty of doing this—but give yourself another careful look. Do you talk about others behind their backs, belittling them or laughing at their foibles? Do you complain about others' actions? Do you avoid certain people because they annoy you—or because you just don't think they're very interesting? All of these behaviors are a form of judgment.

Jesus warned against hurting one of His "little ones" (Matthew 18:6, 10, 14). We often interpret this to mean children, and it certainly includes them—but "little ones" could also be those people who don't seem very important, the people you think it's okay to avoid, complain about, or dismiss. Each of those people is beloved by God—just as you too are beloved.

Point out in me, Lord, any behaviors that indicate I am judging others rather than loving them as You love them. I don't want to set myself outside Your realm of love.

BONDS OF LOVE

The Lord turned the captivity of Job, when he prayed for his friends.
Job 42:10 KJV

When you enter into a love relationship with God, love sets you free. In the process, it changes how you interact with others—and that in turn draws you even closer to God.

Job went through a lot. He lost possessions, family, health, and reputation. His friends weren't much help to him; they told him it was all his fault, rather than giving him sympathy and support. But notice that Job's situation changed when he prayed *for his friends*—those same false friends who had done so little for him when he was in trouble.

When you walk in the love God gives you, you stop manipulating, hurting, and complaining about others. You look past your differences. You no longer care only about the people who think like you do and who support your ideas and opinions; instead, you form new bonds shaped by God's great, inclusive love.

Thank You, Lord, that You love us all. Help me to see past all the differences and irritations and hurts that upset me so much. Teach me to form bonds of divine love with others.

THINK ABOUT GOOD THINGS

It's wonderful what happens when Christ displaces worry at the center of your life. Summing it all up, friends, I'd say you'll do best by filling your minds and meditating on things true, noble, reputable, authentic, compelling, gracious—the best, not the worst; the beautiful, not the ugly; things to praise, not things to curse.

PHILIPPIANS 4:7–8 MSG

Science has found that the cost of anxiety is high. It uses up energy that could be spent far more productively. It takes its toll on our bodies, giving us headaches and stomach problems. Even our immune systems suffer, making us more susceptible to colds and other illnesses. After long enough—when anxiety has become a way of life—it can even contribute to heart disease and high blood pressure. And worrying about the future—focusing on things that may never actually happen—robs us of the present moment's joy.

When Paul encountered this problem in the Philippian church, he gave them the advice in these verses. "When you catch yourselves brooding over your worries," he said, "transform your anxiety into prayer. Make a habit of thinking about good things instead of bad. Focus on all the ways that God has demonstrated His love to you." When you do that, your anxiety will be replaced with God's love and peace.

Dear Lord, You know how easily worries overtake me. Teach me to focus on Your love instead.

POWERFUL PRAYER

Is anyone among you in trouble? Let them pray. . . .
The prayer of a righteous person is powerful and effective.
JAMES 5:13, 16 NIV

Prayer doesn't miraculously take away life's challenges. It's not a magic spell that makes all our troubles go *poof*! Jesus Himself prayed to be delivered from the cross—and yet He was crucified. The apostle Paul prayed to be delivered from his "thorn in the flesh"—but that didn't happen either. Does this mean that God didn't love Jesus and Paul? Absolutely not.

But you may be thinking, *If God didn't answer even Jesus' and Paul's prayers the way they wanted, what's the point of me even trying?* But both Jesus and Paul show us how prayer changed them on the inside, allowing God to use their outer circumstances as opportunities for His love to work in their lives. Prayer was the way both Jesus and Paul struggled with their emotional reactions to life's difficulties—and then, through prayer, they were able to accept God's will for their lives. Even more, their prayer gave God room to transform the meaning of their circumstances, so that pain and hardship became an opportunity for God's love to work in them and through them, changing the world around them.

Through prayer, God's love will do the same in your life.

God, when it seems as though You're not answering my prayers, give me greater confidence in Your love.

THINK LIKE JESUS

Since Jesus went through everything you're going through and more, learn to think like him.
1 PETER 4:1 MSG

How did Jesus think? The way to find out is to examine His life as it is recorded in the Gospels. There you can see Him interacting with others. He is constantly reaching out to the unimportant, forgotten people of the world with the message that they are loved. Just as children cannot grow and thrive without love, the knowledge of love changes lives.

Each day communicate this message both to yourself and to the world around you: *You are loved by God! God loves* you*!* Then stop putting down either yourself or others, because this counteracts your message of love.

Pay attention. When you get pulled into complaining about or insulting others, you not only stop communicating love—you also lose your own awareness of God's love.

Jesus, I want to learn to think like You. Point out anything in me that is getting in the way of Your love.

MORE THAN JUST A WORD

If I speak human or angelic languages but do not have love, I am a sounding gong or a clanging cymbal. If I have the gift of prophecy and understand all mysteries and all knowledge, and if I have all faith so that I can move mountains but do not have love, I am nothing. And if I donate all my goods to feed the poor, and if I give my body in order to boast but do not have love, I gain nothing.

1 CORINTHIANS 13:1–3 HCSB

Sometimes we believe in God's love in an abstract sort of way that does no good, either for ourselves or for the world around us. We believe in the love of God—but we do nothing *for* the love of God. We don't allow it to change our lives from the inside out. We *believe* in God's kingdom of love, but we don't *do* anything for it. We don't work hard to build the kingdom in our little corners of the world.

Love is only a word, just an idea, if the actions meant to accompany it never happen.

Lord Jesus, thank You that You loved me so much You gave Your life for me. Help me now to give my life for You. Show me how to build Your kingdom.

GOD'S ARMS

The God of all grace, who called you to his eternal glory in Christ, after you have suffered a little while, will himself restore you and make you strong, firm and steadfast.

1 PETER 5:10 NIV

What is grace? According to the Greek dictionary, the word used here in the original language has to do with God freely extending Himself toward you, reaching out to you, the way a mother reaches out her arms to catch her toddler. This attitude of love and kindness is not based on any behavior of yours. If it were, that would mean God would pull back His arms if you stopped doing something—but that will never happen.

When a toddler is learning to walk, her mother's love gives her confidence. She knows that if she falls, she'll be picked up and comforted. The mother won't turn and walk away, leaving her child there crying. You can have that same confidence. You can live your life freely, to the full, knowing that should you fall, God will swoop you up into His arms.

Thank You, God, for Your grace that is always reaching out to me. Make me stronger, more settled, more established in Your love—and when I fall, catch me and set me back on my feet.

MORE ROOM FOR LOVE

Think of yourselves the way Christ Jesus thought of himself. He had equal status with God but didn't think so much of himself that he had to cling to the advantages of that status no matter what. Not at all. When the time came, he set aside the privileges of deity and took on the status of a slave, became human! Having become human, he stayed human. It was an incredibly humbling process. He didn't claim special privileges. Instead, he lived a selfless, obedient life and then died a selfless, obedient death.

PHILIPPIANS 2:5–8 MSG

Charles Spurgeon, the nineteenth-century preacher, once said, "If we empty our hearts of self, God will fill them with His love." This is what Jesus did. He emptied Himself of all His rights and privileges as the Son of God. And then He was free to be the incarnation of God, filled to the brim with the love of God.

Jesus, help me to think of myself the way You thought of Yourself. Show me how to empty myself more and more of my arrogance and selfishness. I want to make more room for Your love in my heart.

FREEDOM

By entering through faith into what God has always wanted to do for us. . .we throw open our doors to God and discover at the same moment that he has already thrown open his door to us. We find ourselves standing where we always hoped we might stand—out in the wide open spaces of God's grace and glory, standing tall and shouting our praise.

Romans 5:1–2 msg

Paul, who wrote this passage of scripture, knew from experience how it felt to have doors thrown open, letting him walk free into an open space. He spent some time in prison, not because he had committed any real crime, but because he had offended the religious leaders of his day.

Paul easily could have felt angry and frustrated by his experiences; he could have despaired of ever being able to carry out the big plans he had for bringing the good news of Jesus to the world. But instead, Paul trusted in God's love. And in time, that love set him free.

Do you ever feel like you too are in a prison cell of sorts? Loneliness can feel like a cell. So can illness and failure. You may feel as though you're stuck, unable to do the work you believe God has called you to do. But all the time, there's a doorway in every prison cell you encounter—the doorway of God's love that will set you free.

Lord God, when I feel imprisoned by something in my life, remind me that Your love will set me free.

EVERYTHING!

He that spared not his own Son, but delivered him up for us all, how shall he not with him also freely give us all things?

ROMANS 8:32 KJV

Oswald Chambers, the early twentieth-century evangelist, wrote:

> *If what we call love doesn't take us beyond ourselves, it is not really love. If we have the idea that love is characterized as cautious, wise, sensible, shrewd, and never taken to extremes, we have missed the true meaning. This may describe affection and it may bring us a warm feeling, but it is not a true and accurate description of love.*

The sort of love God demonstrates to us goes to extremes. Not only did God give His Son, but He gives "all things"—*everything*!

So as we grow in this love relationship with God, it makes sense that we too learn to throw caution to the wind. We too need to give God *everything*.

Thank You for Your extravagant, extreme love, Lord. I want to love You the same way.

PRESENTS

So if you sinful people know how to give good gifts to your children, how much more will your heavenly Father give good gifts to those who ask him.
MATTHEW 7:11 NLT

God is your loving parent. And not only that, He is the best parent, the parent who is never too tired, never gets impatient, never feels preoccupied, never runs out of love. He is what human parents try to be like; He's at the root of all father-love and all mother-love—but human love is always an imperfect picture of God's love.

By nature, parents love to give to their children. Parents love the magic of Christmas morning as their children open up their presents. Parents delight in birthday celebrations.

And that's how God feels about you. In His mind, every day is Christmas, every day is your birthday. Every day is a day full of gifts that express His love.

Oh God, thank You for all You give to me. Thank You for being the perfect parent who gives only good gifts.

CARE FOR THE EARTH

May the heavens be joyful, and may the earth rejoice; may the sea roar, and all it contains; may the field be jubilant, and all that is in it. Then all the trees of the forest will sing for joy before the Lord, for He is coming.

PSALM 96:11–13 NASB

The Lord's love spills out into the entire earth, as this verse illustrates—and as we grow in our love relationship with God, our love for the entire earth increases. What God created, He loves, and He loves this blue and green and brown planet on which we all live. Working to protect our planet is one more way we can express our love of God. He calls us to be His hands and feet, working together to do works of love.

"Love My beloved world," God says to us. "I created it. I am the Father of all who live in it. Care for it on My behalf. Love it as one more way of loving Me."

Dear Lord, Your love for me constantly amazes me. Thank You for giving us the earth to be our home, for creating so much beauty. Show me ways to express my love for You by guarding our planet's well-being.

GOD'S TRADEMARKS

"I'm God, and I act in loyal love. I do what's right and set things right and fair, and delight in those who do the same things. These are my trademarks."

Jeremiah 9:24 msg

When you see a trademark, you know that product—whether it's a car, a pair of sneakers, or a book—was made by a particular company. In the same way, whenever you see love and justice at work in the world, you know it's the handiwork of the Lord.

When you look around at the world today, sometimes it's hard to see God's trademarks. You may wonder if He has left us on our own. But keep looking. Sometimes you find those divine marks in the places where you least expect to see them. God loves to take us by surprise!

And remember, we too are called to do God's work. So when we can't see the signs of God's love and justice anywhere we turn, it's time for us to get busy!

Show me where I can do Your work, Lord. I want to bear Your trademark.

PARTAKERS

Wherefore, holy brethren, partakers of the heavenly calling, consider the Apostle and High Priest of our profession, Christ Jesus.

HEBREWS 3:1 KJV

We are "partakers of the heavenly calling"—the call to love—led forward by Christ Jesus. But sometimes, instead of being joyful as partakers of God's love, we act as though we've been called to a life of gloom and doom. We look around at all that is wrong with our world, and we let these things loom larger and larger in our minds. Meanwhile, God seems smaller and smaller.

In reality, though, God is much greater than anything we see in our broken world. When we give Him room to live in our hearts, His love seems to expand in size. Christ Jesus, the full expression of God's love, will look larger and larger.

Lord Jesus, when I start focusing on the world's problems, turn my attention back to You. Remind me to always look at the world through the filter of Your love. Thank You that You allow me to partake in Your calling, the calling of love.

TIME

God has us where he wants us, with all the time in this world and the next to shower grace and kindness upon us in Christ Jesus.
EPHESIANS 2:7 MSG

We often feel as though there's just not enough time. We feel a constant sense of pressure to get more and more accomplished in a limited amount of time.

But that's not how God looks at time. In God's mind, there is always just the right amount of time for Him to do His work of love in the world. He's not rushed, He's not panicked, He's not stressed out. He simply stretches out His love day after day after day.

God's love is so great that it can never be expressed in an instant—or even in a day or an entire year. He needs an entire lifetime, and on into eternity, to show you how much He loves you.

When time seems too short, my God, remind me that time is Your creation—and You made it exactly the right size to hold Your love.

SPIRITUAL EYE STRAIN

God will clear your blurred vision—you'll see it yet!
PHILIPPIANS 3:15 MSG

We all have blurry spiritual eyes at times. We see the bills piling up more clearly than we see our Father's love. We can see our worries about a loved one far more sharply than we can perceive the loving arms of the Lord. Anger and disappointment and despair loom so large that we can't see past them.

If you have times like that, don't worry. God is the divine ophthalmologist. When you turn to Him, He can clear your blurry vision.

God, I have spiritual eye strain. I've been staring so hard at all the things that worry me that now when I try to see Your face, everything seems blurred and fuzzy. Help me, Lord. Clear my vision. I want to be able to see You and Your love again.

TEARS

"He will wipe every tear from their eyes."
Revelation 21:4 NLT

When we experience the sorrow of losing a loved one, it's hard to see or feel God's love. This grief cuts deep into our hearts. Life feels broken. *We* are broken. We don't know how we can continue to live in a world that no longer holds our loved one.

Jesus understands sorrow like this. He too felt it when He was on earth. He will walk with us through each day of sorrow, anger, confusion, denial, and pain as we learn to cope with the loss of a loved one. He will never ask us to hurry and get over it; He understands that grief has its own timeline and can't be rushed.

And through it all, He holds out this hope—one day, when this life is over, He will wipe away every tear.

Jesus, when my heart aches, hold me close. I'm too sad to think, too sad to shape a prayer—but I know You are with me. I trust You.

LOVE IN THE NIGHT

When you lie down, you will not be afraid;
when you lie down, your sleep will be sweet.
PROVERBS 3:24 NASB

Do you ever have insomnia? Sleeplessness can be a terrible thing. It can make you tired and cranky. When you're tired, you're more likely to feel anxious or depressed, more easily angered, less patient. It becomes a vicious cycle: the more upset and tense you become, the less you can sleep; the less you sleep, the more upset and tense you become. You may end up afraid even to go to bed because you don't want to face the frustration you feel when you lie there awake hour after hour. Anxiety can overwhelm you in the darkness, making you feel helpless and full of doubt.

But the Bible tells us that God has compassion on our sleeplessness. He is with us there in the darkness. So the next time you lie awake, tossing and turning, see if you can use the quiet night hours as a time to draw close to God. Let yourself rest in His love. See if you can hear Him singing you His lullaby of love.

Lover of my soul, thank You that Your love is always with me, even in the night when I can't sleep. Help me to relax into Your love. Even if I still can't sleep, may I spend the sleepless hours in Your company, wrapped in Your love.

YOUR CHILDREN

"I'll make sure that your children flourish."
GENESIS 22:17 MSG

God's love for you extends beyond you and flows out into the children in your life. Not only does He use your love for these children as a vehicle for *His* love, but He also loves and blesses your children in ways you are too small to do. You cannot go with your children everywhere they go, and the older they get, the more you'll have to let go of your control over their lives. But God never abandons them. He follows close beside them.

Even when you have passed over into eternity, God will still be loving and blessing your children. He will see that they flourish. He has promised!

Bless my children, Lord. Use my love for them to glorify You. May they see You through my love. And when my love is too small or fails, may they see past me to You. Accompany them all the days of their lives. Make them flourish.

PASSIONATE PATIENCE

We know how troubles can develop passionate patience in us, and how that patience in turn forges the tempered steel of virtue, keeping us alert for whatever God will do next.
ROMANS 5:3–4 MSG

We don't often think of patience as being passionate, but this is what the Bible describes. It's the same "passion" that Jesus brought to the cross, a love that's willing to endure, to wait, to keep going no matter what. This is an active patience, an expectant hope that lasts through all of life's hardships because it *knows* that God's love is at work—and He is always in the process of doing something wonderful.

Lord God, give me passionate patience. Make me willing to wait for Your love. Help me to be confident that You are always working, even when I can't see what You're doing. Teach me to rely on Your love in good times and bad. Keep me alert for what You'll do next. I don't want to miss it!

THE GENEROSITY OF CHRIST

Out of the generosity of Christ, each of us is given his own gift.
Ephesians 4:7 msg

Do you ever feel as though some people have received more blessings than you have? Maybe you look at their beautiful big house. . .or their supersuccessful children. . .or their talents and skills. . .or their beautiful face and figure. Maybe you even feel as though some people are just plain more *spiritual* than you are, as though it comes more easily to them.

We all have those feelings sometimes. But they're lies. Because God never blesses any of His children more than He does the others. We each have our own special gifts, intended just for us. Each of us is uniquely loved. Each is given what we most truly need.

Thank You, Lord Jesus, for the gifts You've given me. Help me not to focus so much on others' blessings but instead put to good use what You've given me. Thank You for Your loving generosity.

I LOVE YOU, LORD!

I love you, Lord; you are my strength.
The Lord is my rock, my fortress, and my savior.
Psalm 18:1–2 NLT

You, God, are all that I need, all that I long for. My God, my helper, I love You for Your great goodness, Your kindness and compassion. I love You for Your amazing creativity, Your wondrous beauty. I love You for making me, for blessing me all through my life. I love You for sending Jesus to show me Your love in physical form.

I know I don't love You as much as I might, but help me to love You as much as I can. I can't love You as You deserve to be loved, for I can't love You more than my own limits permit. Give me a greater capacity to love, though, and I will love You more and more (though never as much as You deserve).

Thank You, beloved Lord, for loving me.

SCRIPTURE INDEX

OLD TESTAMENT

NEW TESTAMENT